The Talented M

'What Phyllis Nagy achieves is the challenging fe...
...ience inside Ripley's mind' *Financial Times*

'...Nagy's thrilling adaptation creates a fine theatrical elaboration of
...ith's narrative' *Daily Mail*

'...ent and gripping' *The Express*

...is Nagy was born in New York City and has lived in London since
...... Her plays, including *Weldon Rising*, *Butterfly Kiss*, *Disappeared*, *The Strip* and
...r Land, have been produced throughout the world and have received
...ards including the Writers' Guild of Great Britain Award, a Mobil Prize, a
...san Smith Blackburn Prize, the Eileen Anderson/Central Television Award,
...wo National Endowment for the Arts Fellowships and a McKnight
Foundation Fellowship. Phyllis is currently under commission to the Royal
Shakespeare Company, Nottingham Playhouse and the Royal Court Theatre,
where she was recently writer-in-residence.

PTO for label

by the same author

Butterfly Kiss*
The Scarlet Letter
Trip's Cinch
The Strip*
Weldon Rising & Disappeared*
Never Land*
Phyllis Nagy Plays: 1*

* *available from Methuen*

THE
TALENTED
MR RIPLEY

by **Phyllis Nagy**

adapted from the novel by **Patricia Highsmith**

Methuen Drama

PUBLISHED BY METHUEN IN 1999

1 3 5 7 9 10 8 6 4 2

First published in the United Kingdom in 1999 by
Methuen Publishing Limited
20 Vauxhall Bridge Road, London SW1V 2SA

Random House Australia (Pty) Limited
20 Alfred Street, Milsons Point, Sydney, New South Wales 2061, Australia
Random House New Zealand Limited
18 Poland Road, Glenfield, Auckland 10, New Zealand
Random House South Africa (Pty) Limited
Endulini, 5A Jubilee Road, Parktown 2193, South Africa

Methuen Publishing Limited Reg. No. 3543167

A CIP catalogue record for this book
is available from the British Library

ISBN 0–413–73220–7

Typeset by Deltatype Ltd, Birkenhead, Merseyside
Printed and bound in Great Britain by
Cox & Wyman Ltd, Reading, Berkshire

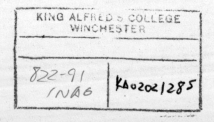

The Talented Mr Ripley

Characters

Tom Ripley, *twenty-five, an utterly compelling, fastidious, charming and measured psychopath.*

Richard Greenleaf, *twenty-five, a rich young man who lacks motivation or real direction. He is, however, a genuinely good soul, utterly lacking in suspicion or cynicism. Is roughly the same height, weight and colouring as Ripley.*

Marge Sherwood, *twenty-five, intelligent, no-nonsense, pretty and wary of Ripley.*

Freddie Miles, *twenty-five, a big, red-headed, good-natured, slow-moving school friend of Richard's.*

Herbert Greenleaf, *Richard's father.*

Emily Greenleaf, *Richard's mother.*

Aunt Dottie, *Tom's aunt.*

Marc Priminger, *Tom's friend.*

Fausto, *a naïve Italian teenager.*

Tenente Roverini, *an Italian police lieutenant.*

Sophia, *a young Italian prostitute.*

Silvio, *a young Italian gigolo.*

Reddington, *a young cartoonist.*

All characters are American unless otherwise noted.

The play is performed by seven actors with the following roles doubled: Freddie Miles/Marc Priminger; Marge Sherwood/ Sophia; Herbert Greenleaf/Roverini; Emily Greenleaf/Aunt Dottie; Fausto/Reddington/Silvio. These doublings are not arbitrary and it is crucial that they be followed exactly.

Time

The play is set in the early 1950s. Within the acts, there is often a multiple time element whereby Ripley operates simultaneously in two scenes which take place in two different time frames. Only Ripley is ever aware of the differing time frames, and sometimes not even he is aware. The other characters know only the present the text presents them with.

Setting

The set should suggest limitless open space and horizon. An enormous ship's compass sits amidst many watercolours painted in differing styles and of various sizes which hang suspended above the stage as if they come from nowhere. The watercolours are all landscapes, and most of them are seascapes of violent, storm-tossed ocean. A small table and two chairs, which are used in various ways and in various scenes, are necessary.

Note on the Text

The use of capitals in certain passages does not necessarily or exclusively indicate a rise in speaking volume. However, capitalisation always suggests a shift in intensity or emphasis. Similarly, the use of beats does *not* indicate the use of pauses. Rather, the beats indicate shifts in thought, sometimes quite abrupt shifts.

The action is meant to be fluid and continuous; the play's structure is not episodic – rather, the whole of both acts should be treated as if they are two complete, extended scenes. There should never be a moment of inactivity or silence unless the text indicates otherwise.

The Talented Mr Ripley was commissioned and first produced by the Palace Theatre, Watford, where it premiered on 2 October 1998, with the following cast (in order of appearance):

Tom Ripley	John Padden
Reddington / Fausto / Silvio	Raph Taylor
Herbert Greenleaf / Roverini	Vincent Marzello
Emily Greenleaf / Aunt Dottie	Patricia Quinn
Marc Priminger / Freddie Miles	David Ganly
Richard Greenleaf	Joseph Millson
Marge Sherwood / Sophia	Lou Gish

Directed by Giles Croft
Designed by Nick Sargent
Lighting by Jon Linstrum
Sound by Scott Myres

Act One

Darkness. The sound of waves and gulls. Gentle. Languorous.
Peaceful. Still. A fishing boat's bell sounds. Gradually, the sound of
the waves becomes more and more unstable and turbulent until it
becomes the sound of a violent storm at sea – a typhoon, an event of
devastating catastrophe. And just at its height, when it seems it can't
get any worse, the storm sounds are replaced by the sound of a
motorboat at full speed – the sound of which appears to come closer
and closer and closer until the lights come up suddenly, the motorboat
sound disappears, and **Tom Ripley** *is there, startling as the storm,*
to address us:

Tom   We live happily ever after under cover. He tells me
this one morning while he butters our toast and she
prepares the espresso. We're at the end of our dock. I say
to him: it's the first sunny morning in months and what do
you *mean* we'll live happily ever after under cover? Just as
I'm about to sink my teeth into a slice of toast, an adder
slithers up my right leg. I am not at all startled, but I
jump. To the left. He drops his toast. To the right. On to
the dock. The toast burns a hole right through the dock.
We watch it smoulder. She says to me: but what about the
adder? I say to her: don't worry, it's domesticated. But
what about the *toast*? We have no more bread. He cries.
Unstoppable tears. The adder's at my jugular, preparing for
a big bite. And I'm thinking, no no no. This can't be.
We're going to live happily ever after under cover. The
water rises. Above the dock. We're knee deep. We're waist
deep. I cannot move. It's his tears, she says, it's his tears
creating a flood. What have you done? What have you
done? The adder's poised to strike. What the hell. We'll
starve anyway. And then I wake.

Reddington *enters. He wears a suit. He's nervous. He pulls at*
his tie.

Reddington   I hope I'm not late. Or early. That would
be terrible, right?

Reddington *sits at a small table.* **Tom** *joins him. An adding machine. An impressive, fat, ominous-looking file folder on the floor near* **Tom**. **Tom** *pours out two cups of coffee while* **Reddington** *speaks.*

Reddington   It's easy to forget your income. I mean, the details of income. You know how it is. Irregular jobs. Distractions. Holidays. Dates. Before you know it, you've lost a few fifties. Here and there.

Tom   Cream?

Reddington   Milk, thanks. So. I was saying. *What* was I saying?

Tom   The loss of a few fifties. Here and there.

Reddington   Well, yeah. Exactly my point. Cartooning isn't what you might call a regular job providing a regular pay cheque.

Tom   Sugar?

Reddington   Three, please. So. I was saying. Cartooning. You know. It's an unreliable source of income. Fun. But unreliable.

Tom   You ought to watch that. It's dangerous, Mr Reddington.

Reddington   What. Comic books?

Tom   Sugar.

Tom *takes one precise sip at his coffee.*

Tom   I'm afraid we're talking about something more significant than a few fifties here and there. According to Internal Revenue records, we're speaking of several thousand dollars of unreported income over the last two years. Three thousand, two hundred and twenty-two dollars and seventy-seven cents. To be precise. After taking certain deductions and exemptions into consideration, that leaves you with tax owing, including late charges, of two hundred dollars and three cents. Which you may now remit via personal cheque made payable to the Internal Revenue Service.

Reddington (*laughs*)   Listen, mister. I'm lucky if I made several thousand dollars in the whole of my *life*.

Tom   Tax records don't lie. And in your case, there are many, many records. (*Beat.*) You're young. Strong. You look strong. There's time.

Reddington   Pardon?

Tom   There's time. To earn several thousand dollars. (*Beat.*) How many dates have you had in the past two years, Mr Reddington? An approximate number will suffice.

Reddington   Geez. I didn't know you guys were interested in –

Tom (*interrupts*)   We're not. You said something earlier. About losing the details of your income through distractions. Holidays. Dates. So. How many dates? How may holidays?

Reddington   What did you say your name was? McMasters? Central office or something?

Tom *picks up a business card from the table and holds it up for* **Reddington** *to read.*

Tom   George McAlpin. Manhattan District Internal Revenue Supervisor.

Reddington *takes the card from* **Tom**, *looks it over himself.*

Reddington   Yeah. You did say that. You did. I'm just, well, nothing like this has ever happened to me before and I'm kinda confused so maybe you could slow down and explain the details a little more clearly so –

Tom   If you'd prefer, I can refer the matter to my own supervisor, who is responsible for the entire Northeast Sector. He's based on Boston, but should get down to New York sometime next month. Of course, that would mean your incurring an additional thirty days or (*He punches some* *numbers into the adding machine.*) twelve dollars and twenty-three cents interest and late charges.

Tom *takes another sip of his coffee.*

Reddington   Isn't it a little weird, a tax collector doing business in a dive on Mulberry Street? Most people work in offices.

Tom   Most people are terribly unhappy. Most people remain hunched over desks, cubicles rife with other people's germs and never even *dream* they will be contacted by the Internal Revenue Service. (*Beat.*) Washington prefers its inspectors to be mobile. No offices, no overhead. We are saving taxpayer dollars, Mr Reddington. You, on the other hand, are so irresponsible as to lose track of your own income. (*Beat.*) Have you taken many holidays over the last two years?

Reddington   Okay. Listen. I'm just a guy who draws comics. I admit, yeah, maybe I don't pay too much attention at tax time. I give you what I think you're owed. That's all. But I don't want trouble. I don't want visits from supervisors and I certainly don't want anybody poking into my vacation preferences. So. Do I make the cheque payable to you?

Tom   Are you attempting to bribe an employee of the Federal Government? Because if you are, Mr Reddington, I shall have to take far more drastic measures. I shall have to report you.

Reddington   Hey, hold on just a – Yeah? You're gonna report me? Who you gonna report me to?

Tom   To ... another department.

Reddington   Which department? Exactly.

Tom   The appropriate department. Would you *like* me to take this further? Would you *like* me to make a telephone call?

Reddington (*backing down*)   Please. Mr McAlpin. I wasn't trying to bribe you. I really wasn't. I just –

Tom (*interrupts*)   Make your cheque payable to the Internal Revenue Service. Two hundred dollars and three cents.

Reddington *writes out a cheque.* **Tom** *sips at his coffee.* **Reddington** *holds out the cheque to* **Tom**.

Tom   Please put the cheque on the table.

Reddington *puts the cheque on the table.* **Tom** *peers over at it, then picks it up, inspects it, puts it down on the table beside him.*

Tom   The United States Government thanks you for your custom.

Reddington   Five dates. I've had five dates in two years. If you're really that interested.

Tom   That's not much of a distraction, is it?

Reddington   Some guys, mostly other guys, have all the luck.

Tom   I'm sure you'd be regarded as quite a catch, Mr Reddington.

Reddington   You think so? Nah. You don't think so.

Tom   But I do. Truly. (*Beat.*) Your day will come, Mr Reddington.

Reddington   Okay. Well. Thanks. I mean, I hope I never see you again, but thanks.

Reddington *rises.* **Tom** *rises.* **Reddington** *holds out a hand to* **Tom**. **Tom** *grasps it firmly in both of his hands, pats* **Reddington**'s *hand as if he's just given him a papal blessing.*

Tom   Keep track of your money, Mr Reddington. You never know when you'll need it. Or when the Internal Revenue will need it.

Tom *releases* **Reddington**'s *hand. He sits down, sips at his coffee as if* **Reddington** *is no longer there.*

Reddington (*laughs*)   So that's it. I can go now. Jeez. I'll

tell you something. You guys sure know how to make a
fella sweat.

Tom   Why, thank you.

Reddington (*still laughing*)   Huh? Yeah, whatever, pal. See
you around. I mean – you know what I mean. Arrivederci.

Tom   Ciao.

Reddington *exits.* **Tom** *pours himself another cup of coffee. He
removes a cigarette case from his jacket, lights a cigarette. He picks up*
Reddington's *cheque from the table, regards it as he smokes. He
burns a hole in the centre of the cheque with the end of his cigarette.
On another part of the stage,* **Herbert Greenleaf** *enters. He
wears a smoking jacket and a cravat. He carries a full glass and a
crystal decanter of port. He sets down the decanter and drinks his
port.* **Tom** *is unaware of* **Herbert**. **Tom** *burns holes in each
corner of the cheque.*

Herbert   Something about your laugh catches my
attention. I *know* I've heard it before. So distinct. Halting.
And oddly incomplete. Stops me in my tracks outside the
cafe. Look inside and the first thing I see is you laughing
with two other men. Whispers. Back slapping. Shoulders
touching. And then it occurs to me who you are. Richard's
friend. Martha's Vineyard. That soccer game. You in goal.
Bruised and bullied and beaten by the others but refusing
to concede a point. Bloodied nose, bandaged head.
Incredible display of nerve. And so I think, yes, why not?
This must be the man for the job. I follow you for days.

Tom (*without looking up from his task*)   I noticed. Three days
it took you. Just to say hello. I was beginning to think you
were shy. Or a cop. But I was never scared. Or uncertain.
I was thrilled. Thrilled to be followed.

Tom *regards his handiwork. He puts out his cigarette and lights a
match. He holds the match to the cheque and watches the cheque burn.
He drops the cheque into an ashtray.* **Emily Greenleaf** *enters.
She wears a classy bathrobe. It's almost – but not quite – classy
enough to pass as proper evening wear. She wears a turban and holds
a glass of port.*

Emily   Well, it was *me*, actually, who remembered your name once you said it. Herbert's not good with names. He's good with port. I can't abide the stuff. It's absolutely vile. (*She takes a swig of port.*) Yes. It *was* the Vineyard, wasn't it? You were such a peculiar young man, Tom. I mean, was it really necessary to take such a beating? And then to appear to *enjoy* all that blood and swelling and, well, I *never*. I suppose it's rude to say so. Oh – I don't know. *Is* it rude? After all, it was a long while ago. Has Herbert told you? I'm very ill, Tom. I'm terminal, in fact.

Tom *rises and effortlessly joins the conversation with the* **Greenleafs**.

Herbert   Emily, please. Tom doesn't need to hear this.

Emily   Yes. He does. (*Beat.*) I've lost my hair. It's not the first thing I've lost and it won't be the last. But I did get a turban in the process. Turbans are fantastic things. Luxurious and sinister. Of course, I could never justify wearing one before . . . this. They're so, I don't know, Ali Baba.

Tom   You look magnificent, Mrs Greenleaf.

Emily   You're *sweet*. Could I interest you in some port?

Emily *holds out her glass to* **Tom**. *He hesitates to take it.*

Emily   You won't catch it.

Tom *takes the glass from* **Emily**, *smiles, downs the port.*

Emily   That's my kind of drinking, Tom. Thank you. What was it you said you did these days?

Tom   I write copy for an advertising agency.

Emily   How interesting. Well. It's *not* interesting, is it? But it's something.

Tom   It's a living.

Herbert   I must apologise for my wife's bluntness. She doesn't mean anything by it.

Tom   I appreciate bluntness. It hits the mark every time.

Emily   What was it you said you did, Tom? Honestly, the mind wanders.

Tom   I'm a reporter for the Associated Press.

Herbert   Emily and I are terribly concerned about Richard. We're concerned for his safety.

Tom   Is he in danger?

Herbert   We don't know. But that's not the point. Does our son have to be in danger for us to be concerned for his safety?

Emily   I'd like to see Richard again before I pop my clogs.

Herbert   There really isn't the need for vulgarity, Emily.

Emily   I'm sure Tom is comfortable with my vulgarity. Aren't you, Tom?

Tom   I don't mind. I'm easy.

Emily   See? He's easy. Let's all be easy. Where is your office, Tom? Midtown? Downtown?

Tom   General Electric headquarters. But being a freezer salesman, I'm mostly door-to-door.

Herbert   We last had a letter from Richard two months ago.

Emily   It was a telegram, actually. Dear Mom and Dad. Stop. I'm never coming home. Stop. I'm never coming home. Stop. I'm never –

Herbert   Don't be melodramatic, Emily. (*To* **Tom**.) Richard made it quite clear he had no intention of returning to assume his duties in the family shipyard.

Emily   Can you imagine why *not*, Tom? The lure of the docks. The salt-water. The long, lonely hours. My hair's fallen out into the sea, Tom.

Herbert Richard doesn't know his mother's . . . unwell.

Emily Dying. Say it, Herbert. He doesn't know his mother is about to drop dead. (*Beat.*) More port, Tom?

Tom I wouldn't mind, thanks.

Emily Herbert.

Emily *takes* **Tom**'s *glass, holds it out to* **Herbert**. **Herbert** *fills the glass.* **Emily** *takes a long swig.*

Emily I really can't fathom how anybody can drink the stuff. Here you are, Tom. Who would have guessed it? Tom Ripley. A military man. I'm so proud.

Tom I'm a pharmacist, Mrs Greenleaf. Not a soldier.

Emily Of course you are. I'm so silly. Forgive me. I'm dying.

Tom *takes the glass from* **Emily**. *He drinks.* **Herbert** *drinks. An awkward pause.*

Herbert We have a proposition for you, Tom.

Tom Sounds serious.

Emily It's Herbert's proposition. So it's bound to be serious. Earthbound. Humourless.

Herbert Emily, for God's sake will you please – (*He gathers control of himself.*) The medication. It's quite hard on her system. And sometimes, rarely, the pain causes her to – it blurs her sense of discretion and it – she speaks out of – she can be cruel. She can be terribly cruel.

Emily What my husband means to say is: pay no attention to me. And sadly, I find I must agree with him.

Herbert I'd like you to, that is, Emily and I would like you to – would you consider taking a trip to Italy on our behalf, Tom? Would you try to convince Richard to come home?

Tom Well, the precinct rota may not permit a trip at this time. Crime waits for no detective, Mr Greenleaf.

Herbert   We will pay all of your travel expenses and provide a generous stipend for, let's say, two months. And if it should become necessary for you to stay a bit longer, well, then, I'm sure we would come to some agreement on further remuneration.

Tom   I see.

Herbert   And it goes without saying that we will provide first-class passage across the Atlantic. No expense will be spared, Tom.

Tom   Water. I see.

Herbert   I would be, that is, Emily and I would be eternally grateful should you decide to take up our proposition.

Tom (*after a pause*)   Richard gave me a black eye that day in goal. I've always admired him. I'd like to do the right thing by you, Mr Greenleaf. I'll go to Italy. I'll send Richard home.

Herbert   God bless you, Tom.

Emily *takes off her turban and drops it to the floor. She's bald.*
Marc Priminger *enters. He's a prim little man who wears a bow tie. He carries an open umbrella.*

Marc   God bless you, Tom.

Emily   Surprise. Surprise.

Marc   Lord only knows what I might have done had you not *gallantly* turned round that corner with your big bold umbrella.

Emily *begins to cry.* **Herbert** *goes to her, wraps his arms around her.*

Herbert   Never mind, Emily. Never mind. Herbert's here.

She cries even louder.

Tom   Rivers of tears. The waters rise.

Marc Oh, Tom, you've not been attending those Baptist services again, have you?

Tom Never mind.

Herbert Never mind, darling.

Herbert *leads* **Emily** *off.* **Tom** *picks up her turban and as they pass by he puts it gently back on to* **Emily***'s head.* **Tom** *gives his port glass to* **Herbert***. They exit, and* **Tom** *joins* **Marc** *under the umbrella.* **Tom** *threads his arm through* **Marc***'s.*

Marc Some boys are entirely too lucky.

Tom Well. I *am* doing them a favour.

Marc Can it be so hard? Coercing an old friend into visiting his parents?

Tom That's the thing. He's not an old friend. In fact, he's not a friend at all. I met him once. Cleo Dobelle's wedding. Richard made a pass at the bride. The groom took a swipe, would have flattened Rickie had I not held him back. Spent the rest of the evening nursing poor Rickie Greenleaf back to sobriety. Haven't seen him since. But his folks are convinced I'm somebody I'm not.

Marc Sweet bejesus. I wish somebody tall and wealthy would mistake me for somebody I'm not. Like I said, Tommy. Some boys got too much luck.

Tom Funny thing is, I remember him so well. The way he carried himself. Even when totally smashed.

Marc The rich have a nasty habit of carrying themselves well in most situations.

Tom It was more than that. It was . . . like a light. Like a certainty that would not be denied.

Marc They're like racehorses, Tom. The best ones got the best genes and they ride like the *wind.*

Tom He had an easy way with conversation. An ability to listen without listening and make you feel like a million bucks in the process. And I *knew* all the while I was boring him to death and yet I couldn't help feeling flattered by the bastard. (*Beat.*) Anyway, I couldn't disappoint his parents, could I? They've put their trust in me.

Marc   Their trust *fund*, more like it.

They laugh.

Tom   Anyway, if it hadn't been me, it'd been somebody else.

Marc   Ain't that always the way, Amen.

The sound of the motorboat in the distance. **Marc** *pulls up his collar.*

Marc   Mighty chilly evening. Mighty wet.

Tom   Yeah. But it's gonna be dry as hell at my Aunt Dottie's.

Marc   Whoops. I think you'd best drop me on some neutral street corner well before you approach the gates of hell.

Aunt Dottie *enters. She wears a pristine white apron and carries a feather duster. She dusts. Anything and everything.*

Aunt Dottie   *Where* is it exactly you say you're going, Tom?

Tom   Mongibello.

Marc   Mongibello. Lovely.

Aunt Dottie   And where is *that*? Honestly, Tom, it sounds like a disease.

The motorboat sound comes closer.

Tom   Italy. Blue seas. White sand. A sun that always shines.

Aunt Dottie   You can get that at Coney Island in July. There's no need to investigate foreign *legions*.

Marc   Mmmm. Sounds hot. And sticky. And . . . *stop* me before I commit a cardinal sin of thought.

The motorboat sound becomes a terrifying thunderclap. It really begins to pour. **Marc** *gathers his jacket around his shoulders.*

Marc This is my stop, Tommy. Good luck with Medusa. Oh – listen. You ever hear of a guy called George McAlpin?

Tom McAlpin. Nope. Can't say I have.

Marc An *extremely* brawny detective from the fraud squad of the New York City Police Department – thank you very *much* – dropped by to make a few inquiries. Seems this Mr McAlpin's been using our humble tenement walk-up as a mail drop for illegal activities of the Internal Revenue kind. You know, defrauding widows and priests and schoolteachers of hundreds of *thousands* of dollars.

Aunt Dottie Protection. You'll need all sorts of pills, Tom. That part of the world is simply *not* civilised.

Tom Sounds fun.

Marc Yeah, well, if you see him lurking in our hallway, tell him he's a *damned* fool 'cause he ain't cashed any of his ill-gotten cheques. And if doesn't want the cash, then brother, this southern beau will take it off his sinful hands and offer *absolution*.

And **Marc***'s off. The sound of the rain subsides as* **Tom** *joins his* **Aunt Dottie***. He shuts the umbrella. He watches her dust.*

Aunt Dottie I'm not sure you'll find Catholic churches over there, so I'll pack two rosaries – no, three – and a novena card.

Tom Aunt Dottie. I'm going to Italy. For goodness sake, the Pope lives in Italy. Of course there are Catholic churches.

Aunt Dottie How do I know that? I've never been there. Have you ever been there?

Tom No, Auntie. You know very well I've never been to Italy. I've never been abroad.

Aunt Dottie   Well, there you have it. Propaganda.
European propaganda. I wish you'd reconsider this trip,
Tom.

Tom   It's only for a couple of months.

Aunt Dottie   A couple of months is enough time in
which to contract dysentery or . . . malaria. *Polio*, for all I
know.

Tom   Don't be ridiculous, Auntie. Difficult as that must
be for you.

Aunt Dottie   There is unsophisticated plumbing over
there, Tom. The Germans and Japanese blew all of the
allied . . . facilities . . . to smithereens in the war. So, for
instance, the English have hired the French and the Italians
to dig emergency what-have-yous. And if the French and
Italians are off digging what-have-yous for the English, then
who do you suppose is digging what-have-yous for the
Italians?

Tom   Well I don't know, Aunt Dottie. Probably the
Africans. That sounds just about right in your theory.

Aunt Dottie   Italy. Africa. Wherever. Over *there*. It makes
no difference.

Tom   There are *bathrooms* in Europe, Auntie. And they
work. I won't listen to this foolishness.

Aunt Dottie   Well, Tom. Listen to *this* foolishness: your
allowance is hereby cut off. My thirty dollars a month,
which just about keeps you afloat in the lazy no account
manner to which you've grown accustomed, is no longer
yours to fritter away.

Tom   But Auntie, I depend on –

Aunt Dottie   Be quiet, Tom. I swore to your poor
parents you'd never go hungry. On your momma's
deathbed she said to me, Dottie, you watch my boy gets
enough bread. That's what she said and that's what I've
always done. But you're a grown man now, Tom, not a

boy, and I'm not getting any younger. I need what I earn.

Tom   But you don't work.

Aunt Dottie   I earn interest.

Tom   This is silly. My parents set up a trust fund. It's *my* money.

Aunt Dottie   Two hundred dollars. That was your trust fund. And it ran out ten years ago. There wasn't much investment potential for two hundred dollars in the middle of the depression. Your daddy, whatever else he *might* have been – and Lord knows my sister loved him till it killed her – was a no-good, two-bit schemer. And that kind don't make it a habit of providing for their young. But I honour your momma's memory because she was sweetness and light personified, Tom. She had a crooked, generous grin. And I have always wished for you to take after her. I wonder if you do. (*Beat.*) Anyway, your new magazine job pays well enough, I'd guess. And when *was* it you took up photography, Tom? Remind me.

Tom   But I haven't budgeted for – well, until I'm on my feet I'll need every cent I can get. I mean, it's expensive, living in Europe.

Aunt Dottie   But I thought you said it was civilised over there. Should be easy finding a civilised place to live in a civilised country.

Tom   Civilisation is no assurance of comfortable, inexpensive accommodation.

Aunt Dottie   Yes. Well. My American dollars wouldn't do you any good over there. They don't use real money.

Tom   Would you *please* stop saying 'over there'. Like it's some – some – JUST STOP. JUST SHUT. UP.

Tom *raises his umbrella as if to strike her with it – thinks better of it. An awkward pause as* **Tom** *composes himself and* **Aunt Dottie** *stops dusting to watch him.*

Tom   I'm sorry. I'm really . . . devastated.

Aunt Dottie   Tom Ripley. Have you been standing there all this time with your umbrella dripping ghastly *ghastly* water on my newly polished floors?

Tom   Aunt Dottie. Please. I'm so very, very sorry ... I can't tell you how ... I lost my ... please accept my deepest apologies. Please accept –

Aunt Dottie   It took me twelve hours over two days to polish that floor, Tom Ripley. Have you no decency? Are you an *animal*?

Tom   I'm an animal. Yes. Forgive me.

Aunt Dottie   You were not raised in a barn.

Tom   I was not raised in a barn.

Aunt Dottie   You were not raised in *Italy*.

Tom   No. Nor Italy. You're right.

Aunt Dottie   You are a *pig*, sometimes, Tom Ripley. Your mother is turning in her grave.

Tom   Oink oink.

Aunt Dottie   Now you give me that umbrella and you stand right there until I get back with some rags. We're going to get down on our knees and do some *polishing*, Tom. You stay there, now. Stay.

Aunt Dottie *takes the umbrella from* **Tom**. *She exits. The sound of the gentle waves returns.* **Tom** *addresses the audience. Throughout the following, the light dims progressively, until only* **Tom**'s *head is visible. Also, the sound of the waves is gradually replaced with an upbeat samba.*

Tom   In a variation of my dream, we're on the dock. He and she and I. Except she is not who she is. She's Aunt Dottie. She's whacking the backs of my knees with a six-foot-long umbrella. He and I, we're naked at the edge of the dock squinting out at the sun. We're happy and we're laughing. Laughing. But the umbrella against my legs is hot. Too hot. He says: look, there are nails running all

along the length of that umbrella, but we'll all live happily
ever after under cover. She's furious because the nails don't
draw blood. They draw *water*. The harder she hits, the
more water she draws. Get down on your knees, on your
knees with me, she screams. With me. But it's no use. The
water rises. He and I, we float above it. We hold hands
and we walk on air. But she, she is glued to the dock, her
knees like webbing, the webbing like coarse rope, tying her
down, dragging her under. And yet. And still. The beating
never stops. But her breath ceases. And he and I, we live
happily ever after. With Aunt Dottie under cover.

Lights up abruptly. By now, the samba is in full progress. **Tom** *is
surrounded by luggage. A young Italian man,* **Fausto**, *wears a
scanty swimsuit. He dances around* **Tom** *in a circle.* **Tom** *is
clearly overdressed. He sweats. He takes a handkerchief from his
pocket and wipes his brow.*

Fausto   Hey, Signor. Americano? Ciao, bubby. You
maybe want a room by the sea? Come see with me, bubby.
Come see with Fausto.

Fausto *picks up some of* **Tom**'s *luggage.*

Tom   Don't do that – hey, no. Cut it out. No help. You
understand me? NO HELP.

Fausto   Mister needs a good hotel. Mister bubby sees
with Fausto a good hotel. Che da sul mare.

Tom   Buddy.

Fausto   Eh?

Tom   Buddy. Not *bubby*.

Fausto (*laughs*)   That's funny, mister. Bud-dy.
BUUUUDDDY.

Tom   Yes. Yes, that's right.

Fausto   Fausto will be your buddy. Fausto will find good
hotel. Up the hill. Sea view. Breeze.

Tom (*struggles to take the luggage from* **Fausto**)   There's really no need for you –

Fausto *drops the luggage, grabs* **Tom**'s *hand in both of his own hands. He drops to one knee, holds his head to* **Tom**'s *hand, as if in supplication.*

Fausto   Please, signor, please. I beg you. I take you. I find you very very nice. I find you room.

Tom *pulls his hand away from* **Fausto**. *A pause.* **Tom** *lights a cigarette.* **Fausto** *remains on his knees. The samba has now become a cha-cha.*

Tom   Where's that music coming from?

Fausto   The house. Please. I do jobs. Any jobs. Handy jobs. Buddy.

Tom   There's another American here. In town. A man. Can you help me find him?

Fausto   In the house. Si. Americano.

Tom   The house with the music.

Fausto   Signor Rickie's music. Signor Rickie's house of music. See. Fausto takes you there.

Tom   Get up, please.

Fausto   Fausto kneels. Fausto begs. Fausto stays until signor says si si SI.

Tom   All right. Si. Come on. Get up.

Tom *offers his hand to* **Fausto**. **Fausto** *takes it, gets up.*

Fausto   Fausto wants cigarette. Please. Cigarette. Fausto much obliged.

Tom (*starts to take a cigarette out of his case*)   Where is Signor Rickie's house of music, Fausto?

Fausto   No no no – this one. Fausto wants *this* cigarette.

Fausto *takes* **Tom**'s *half-smoked cigarette from* **Tom**'s *lips.* **Tom** *is not fazed. He lights himself another cigarette.* **Fausto** *inhales deeply. He coughs. He inhales deeply again.*

Fausto Smoking, it's so dirty. Stupendo. Fausto thanks you. I go. Fausto hurries. Bye bye.

Fausto *runs off with one of* **Tom**'*s bags.*

Tom Hold on – hey – that's my bag you've got –

Tom *starts after him, but almost instantly,* **Richard Greenleaf** *appears carrying* **Tom**'*s bag. A reluctant* **Fausto** *is in tow.*

Richard Yours, I take it.

Richard *sets down the bag.*

Tom Yes, thanks. He took off like a shot. I was lighting a cigarette and before I could –

Richard I *know*. He does two, maybe three cigarette tricks a month. What have you got to say to the gentleman, Fausto?

Fausto Mi dispiace. I sorry. Take pity on Fausto. Buddy.

Fausto *bows deeply to* **Tom**.

Richard Don't milk it, Fausto. Scram.

Fausto Okay okay – I go. I scram.

Tom Just a minute. We have unfinished business.

Fausto *stops in his tracks.*

Richard You're not going to press charges, are you? He's really just a kid.

Tom I'm not interested in pressing charges.

Tom *takes out his wallet, removes several thousand lire and gives it to* **Fausto**.

Tom You owe me a trip to the hotel.

Fausto (*can't believe his luck*) Si, hotel. Molto gentile, grazie. Grazie, signor. We go. Best room. Sea breezes. Many beautiful women.

Richard He's looking for a hotel, Fausto, not a brothel.

Tom   Anywhere we can get a pitcher of gin and tonics? This heat, well, it was pretty chilly when I left New York.

Richard   Oh, sure. Sure. Fausto – rouse Signor Morelli from his stupor and tell him to fix us up a pitcher of drinks. Lots of ice. Lots of gin.

Fausto *runs off.*

Richard   I don't know what Fausto has in mind for you, but I'd recommend the Miramare. Not much of a sea breeze, but the view's pretty special.

Tom   Sounds perfect. Let me pay you for the drinks.

Richard   Never mind. Morelli runs the Miramare. He keeps a tab for me. (*Beat.*) Thanks for throwing a few bucks Fausto's way. He doesn't mean anything by his tricks.

Tom   I don't mind. It was a good trick.

Richard   It *is* good, isn't it? He always returns the luggage. Takes him a few days, but all he really wants is to see some poor fool American tourist struggle on the beach without his shoes.

Tom   Well. That would be me.

Tom *extends his hand to* **Richard**.

Tom   Tom Ripley.

Richard   Pleased to meet you. So you're a New Yorker.

Tom   By way of San Antonio. Yes.

Richard   I'm impressed. A Texan.

Tom   Well, I was only there a short while. My father's a diplomat. We move house more often than I have birthdays. Well, *they* move, that is. My parents. I honestly don't remember where they're stationed now. Can't keep track. Me, I settled on New York and never looked back.

Richard   It's a wise man who loses his parents along the way. Wish I could say I was wise. I'm healthy and wealthy.

Tom   Two out of three. (*Beat.*) Can't hide your accent, anyway. Distinctly Yankee.

Richard   Distinctly Park Avenue. Via Martha's Vineyard.

Tom   That's a pretty impressive set of accents.

Richard   Only a long horn's impressed by Park Avenue.

Tom (*shrugs*)   A fella can't help his genes.

Richard   Don't I know it. My father builds boats. Big boats. Full of cherry wood and brass and oh God if I never smell french polish or sea salt again I'll die a happy man. I hate the sea but wouldn't you know I have a talent for two things and one of them's sailing.

Tom   And here you are, surrounded by the sea. (*Beat.*) I can't even swim.

Richard   Funny place to choose for a holiday if you can't swim. Well. You're in the right place for a couple of lessons.

Tom   I'm not on holiday. (*Beat.*) Would you teach me? To swim?

Richard   Maybe. I don't know. Been a while since I've been asked.

Tom   I could pay.

Richard   And I don't need your money. Believe me. (*Beat.*) You're not a tourist. So. What are you?

Tom   I'm a collector.

Richard   Taxes? Jeez, I hope not. Haven't paid mine in two, three years.

Tom   Art. Renaissance sculpture. Relief or otherwise. I'm meandering. Through Italy.

Richard   No kidding. I paint. Landscapes. Or I try to. I think I'm not untalented.

Tom   So that would be your other talent. If one talent's for sailing. (*Beat.*) You look talented.

Richard   Hey – and you should know. Being a collector.

The cha-cha has become a rumba.

Tom (*refers to the music*)   Is there a . . . dance band nearby?

Richard (*laughs*)   Now, that's an idea. But, uh, no such luck. I have a friend who's fond of Arthur Murray.

Tom   Pardon?

Richard   You know, Arthur Murray. (**Tom** *doesn't know.*) A little cha-cha, a little rumba, a little follow-the-painted footsteps . . . ?

Tom (*smiles*)   Sorry. You've lost me.

Richard   Guess the twentieth century's not your forte. (*Beat.*) What's up with Fausto and our drinks? You think Morelli's distilling the gin?

Tom   Look, I'm happy to find Signor Morelli myself. It's no trouble.

Richard   Well . . . maybe you should, if you don't mind. Perhaps Fausto stumbled over some more luggage. It's just over the hill.

Tom   No problem.

Richard   And tell old man Morelli I'll pay up at the end of the week. I owe him a bundle and God knows he's good to me, waiting for my trusty trust-fund wire every month.

Tom   Who are you?

Richard   What?

Tom   Your name. You haven't told me your name.

Richard   Oh. Right. I'm Rickie Greenleaf. And, listen, when you're settled into the Miramare, why don't you drop by for cocktails and a snack. I can't promise much, but I've got the best wine cellar in Mongibello.

Tom   Greenleaf. Greenleaf. I wonder if – no. Never

mind. But maybe – no, no. It's silly. Probably a coincidence. Yes, that'll be it.

Richard   Hey. I love a good coincidence. Try me.

Tom   If I were to say ... Martha's Vineyard. Twelve, fourteen years ago. An early October afternoon. Indian summer. A soccer game. Varsity versus junior varsity. I'm in the J.V. goal. I'm not a good soccer player. In fact, I can't play at all. But a boy's got to earn his letter and I figure, there's nothing wrong with parking my young ass on a bench. I've infinite reserves of patience. So. There I am. Ready to park and cheer. But there's an injury to the goalie. And I am the only reserve.

Richard   Do I *know* you?

Tom   Coach hands me the ball and says, young man, all you've got to do is stand in goal and defend your team's position. I stand in goal. For a long time it's okay, you know, with the offence impossibly keeping the ball down the other end and I'm thinking, well, this isn't so bad. I'm still standing. I'm still here.

Richard   Did you go to *Choate*?

Tom   And then it happens. The varsity charge begins. Seven, maybe eight boys headed my way and the closer they get, the taller I stand in that goal, the less fear I feel. I want them to attack. I *need* their attack in order to experience courage. As if danger, the certain threat of physical violence, galvanizes me. And it's ... electric. And so that day I'm beaten and bruised and kicked to within an inch of my life. The tallest striker attempts a header but I block the shot with my own head and the striker comes flying at me, sends me careening into the goal post. I see stars, but I will not concede a goal.

Richard   I played centre half for Choate varsity. I don't remember this.

Tom   Miraculously, we score. It's not our fault. The varsity right wing, so shocked by the quality of the fight we

put up, scores an own goal on what should have been a
routine save for the goalie. We win. For the first and last
time.

Richard   There was *one* game we lost to the J.V. I think.

Tom   You think right, Rickie. Now think again. Think
about the embarrassment, the absolute shame of handing a
game to a bunch of no-hope freshmen. And the *goalie*.
Think about what it felt like to be beat by a chubby,
pimply *loser* of a bookworm.

Richard   It's really not ringing any bells.

Tom   No? Okay. Think about walking off the field, ready
for the showers, ready for a harangue from coach, ready
for your girlfriend to dump you for the point guard on the
basketball team, ready for your father to weep over the
shame of *his son*, his heir, the receptacle of all of his athletic
talent – losing. Lost. Over.

Richard   I think I remember this.

Tom   Yes. Yes, you do. And now . . . run. Run as if your
life depends on it towards the J.V. goal, where there's a
celebration in progress. Where there's a certain fat kid
being lifted, *hoisted*, far above his teammates' shoulders. It's
the only lift he's gonna get that's not stuck inside his shoes.

Richard   Yeah, yeah – arrogant little snot-nosed fat
sonofabitch. I see him there. Sure.

Tom   And you're running. You're flying towards that goal
and like the bull that you are, you plough into that crowd
of sissy-ass freshman cowards, you *ram* those suckers until
fat boy falls back into his own goal and then – then you go
to work, Rickie. You go to *town*. You take him by his neck
and you –

Richard (*interrupts*)   – And I take him by his neck by his
stupid sweaty disgraceful neck and I raise my fists and I
punch and I punch and his face sinks it collapses into the
dirt and I'm not I'm not going to take it no no no I'm not
gonna take this SHIT this CRAP this GARBAGE from my

FATHER from my SHIT FATHER AND I AIN'T
GONNA NO NO NO I PUNCH I PUMMEL I I I – – –
I PULVERISE THE BASTARD. (*Beat; he realizes he's lost
control.*) I pulverise the poor bastard.

Tom   And that poor black-and-blue bastard was me.

Fausto *runs on, out of breath.*

Tom   Ah, Fausto. You made it back. But where's our G
and Ts?

Fausto   Signor Morelli, he is not there. Signora Morelli,
she is not there. Very quiet. Very empty. I look.
Everywhere. I see. Nobody. Never happen before. Fausto
can no explain.

Tom   Don't worry. Some things are inexplicable.

Richard   There's a reason for everything. There's logic.

Marge Sherwood *enters on to another part of the stage. She's
dressed quite stylishly. She dances in place to the rumba. The others
take no notice of her.*

Marge   Now you explain to me why such a handsome
man should be cursed with two left feet, Tom.

Richard   I could swear it was Freddie Miles. In goal that
day. Fat Freddie.

Tom   I'm afraid not, Rickie. Fat Freddie was the injured
goalie. I was his substitute.

Marge   For two months he's done little else but teach you
to swim and walk down the hill to the post office to collect
his monthly wire payment. And now, it seems he's far more
interested in reading maps of Greece with you than in
learning the finer moves with me. There is no justice in
this world, Tom. None at all. (*Dancing along to the music.*)
And a *one* and a *two* and a three four *five*.

Richard   Well. It's a little late, but. Sorry I hurt you.

Tom   You beat me. To a pulp.

Richard   Jeez, it really was bad, wasn't it?

Tom   Absolutely unforgivable.

A pause. **Tom** *laughs.* **Richard** *laughs.* **Fausto** *laughs. They can't stop laughing.*

Marge (*still dancing*)   We made all these *plans*. Watercolour Week in Capri. Vesuvius Watch in Naples. The Black Hand Hill-Walk through Palermo. Sunshine and Cocktails tour of San Remo. It was like pulling teeth, him agreeing to that trip. And now, well. I'd be lucky to pull him off that chair. I honestly don't know anymore. I give up.

Richard (*through his laughter*)   You gave up.

Tom (*through his laughter*)   I gave up.

Fausto (*through his laughter*)   Signor give up.

Their laughter subsides. The rumba becomes a slow foxtrot. **Marge** *stands, hands on hips.*

Marge   Are you going to *move* off that lethargic backside anytime soon, Rickie?

Richard   Fausto – take Signor Ripley's luggage to the house.

Fausto   Si. Right away, buddy. Right away.

Fausto *collects* **Tom**'*s luggage.*

Tom   That's really not necessary. The hotel Miramare will be fine.

Marge   What's a girl got to do to get a rise out of you, Rickie Greenleaf? Tell me what's necessary, Tom. You probably know. I'm all ears.

Richard   You heard Fausto. The Morellis have vanished. So the hotel's momentarily closed for business. And under the circumstances, it's the least I can do. I insist.

Marge   Go on, Tom. I insist.

Tom   Well, if you insist.

Fausto *exits struggling with* **Tom***'s luggage.*

Marge   Oh, forget it. You've waited so long I've changed my mind. Just . . . never mind.

Richard   Excellent. I'll have Marge rustle us up a couple of G and Ts. I'm *sure* she bought us a big block of ice from the hotel this morning. Come on, Tom. It's just this way.

Richard *starts off.*

Tom   Marge. Who's *Marge?*

But **Richard** *has entered into* **Marge***'s space. He takes her into his arms and they smile sweetly at each other. They dance a foxtrot.* **Richard***'s not very good at all, but gives it his best shot.* **Tom** *addresses the audience.*

Tom   The most careful planning doesn't allow for every possibility. In fact, it's always the thing you pay least attention to that defeats you. And that thing was her. Marge. Name like a grazing cow. And a mind like a . . . shipwreck. Scattered and waterlogged and always at the bottom of everything. With the sludge and the slime and the – (*He catches himself.*) Pretty enough, if you like that sort of thing. I didn't know. How could I know. I wasn't warned. I was not. Prepared. She entered the equation and then. Then the dream started.

Marge   See? It's a piece of cake when you put your mind to it.

Richard   I look a fool. Don't I look a fool, Tom?

Tom (*entering the scene*)   I don't know. I think you look quite graceful. Like Fred Astaire.

Richard   I do?

Marge   I've been *trying* to tell you that for months, honey.

Richard   You've never said any such thing. Has she said any such thing, Tom?

Tom   I can't recall.

Marge   Aren't you two rich. Must have lost all your brain cells on that day trip to Naples. Or was it the weekend in Corsica.

Tom   Could have been the excursion to Verona.

Richard   Oh, yes. It could have been. Didn't we lose an awful lot of grey matter in Verona?

Marge   Very funny. I get a lousy pizza at the Miramare, he gets three days at the leaning tower of Pisa.

Richard *breaks away from the dance. The music stops abruptly.*

Richard   I'm bored. Aren't you bored, Tom?

Marge   Why do you have to ask *him* to verify everything?

Richard   What's for dinner? (*Beat.*) See. Didn't ask him that.

Marge   I don't know what's for dinner because I'm not cooking.

Tom   We'll go out. My treat.

Richard   Marge, baby –

Marge   Don't even try it. And Fred Astaire's practically a relic. So I wouldn't be too flattered by the comparison if I were you.

Tom   I meant no harm, Marge.

Marge   Shouldn't you be moving on soon, Tom? I mean, a busy art dealer like you. Surely Mongibello's charms have worn a little thin.

Tom   I'm not a dealer. I'm a collector.

Marge   Golly. Stupid me. Of course, you must have saved up plenty of cash for the collection over the past couple of months because I sure as hell haven't noticed you forking out for as much as a *napkin* in this place.

Richard   Marge. That's crass.

Tom   She's upset. It's perfectly understandable.

Richard   Really? Well explain it to me, then, because I'm having a pretty tough time understanding her lately.

Marge   Don't talk about me as if I'm not here.

Tom   Look, Rickie. The house is comfortable enough for two, but three is a stretch. She's right. Perhaps I've outstayed my welcome here.

Richard   It's my house. Not hers. You stay as long as you like.

Marge   I AM IN THE GODDAMNED ROOM. HELLO. KNOCK-KNOCK.

Tom   No. You two ought to spend some time together. Alone. I understand Marge's position. She wants her boyfriend's sole attention. It's natural.

Richard   What are you talking about? Marge and me, we're not – I mean, it's good fun but – it's only, well, you know. We're here. Now. That's all.

An awkward silence.

Marge   Would you . . . possibly run that one by me again. I'm not sure I believe what I heard.

Tom   I'll go now. I'm hungry.

Marge   We're all hungry, Tom. Stay. Stay where you are. (*Beat.*) Start talking, Rickie. Please. Before I lose my mind.

Richard   I've been thinking.

Marge   Good. That's a start.

Richard   I mean. We spend lots of time together.

Marge   People who are involved in a relationship often spend lots of time together. So far, so good.

Richard   Are we in a relationship? Is that what this is?

Marge   We cook each other meals. We sometimes share a toothbrush. We've seen each other the morning after. I'd call that a relationship.

Richard   Okay. All right. You're right.

Marge   Thank you. And?

Richard   And ... maybe we should – maybe we
shouldn't –

Marge   You're driving me crazy with all this maybe-we-
should-or-shouldn't bullshit. MAKE UP YOUR MIND.

Richard   We shouldn't.

A silence.

Tom   I'll find Fausto. He owes me an Italian lesson.

Marge   You will NOT GO. (*Beat.*) Anyway, why bother
learning the language when you're going to turn right back
around on a boat to the States?

Tom   I never turn right back around.

Richard   Tom and I thought we'd – there's a sculpture
tour of – well, we're planning a trip to the Greek islands.

Marge   I see.

Tom   There's a dealer in Mykonos I've been
corresponding with for a few months. Several rare pieces
have come his way.

Richard   I've always liked the idea of an art appreciation
tour.

Marge   I didn't know.

Tom   The idea occurred to us last week in Genoa.

Richard   We saw a travelling exhibition. Antiquities.

Tom   It's just one of those things. A simple idea that
takes hold at the right time.

Richard   Tom knows an excellent watercolourist in
Athens. Maybe he'll give me a few lessons. If he thinks I
have promise.

Marge   Promise. That's a risky proposition.

Tom   But worth the risk, don't you think?

Richard   We thought we'd leave in a month's time. Directly after the New Year.

Tom   Passage is relatively inexpensive.

Richard   Weather's not bad.

Marge   I just – will you please just tell me – I only ever meant – I . . . I'll just collect a few things and be out of your way. (*Beat.*) Fausto's at the Miramare, Tom. If you still need him, that is.

Marge *exits.* **Richard** *calls after her.*

Richard   Marge – don't leave it like this – please come out with us.

Tom   Don't.

Richard   But I can't watch her like this. It's like I've stuck a knife right into her heart and –

Tom (*interrupts*)   The pain is hers. Allow her the dignity of keeping it to herself.

Richard   That's a good one. Keep telling me that.

Tom   The vulnerable become strong only by learning to live with their pain. If you comfort Marge now, you'll make it that much harder for her to get along by herself once you leave.

Richard   I thought vulnerability was an asset.

Tom   Pain is an asset. Vulnerability is what your enemies exploit. For instance.

Tom *picks up a small knife from the table. He holds it up for* **Richard** *to see, then pushes the knife edge up against his own wrist.*

Richard   Look Tom, this is not the time for practical jokes.

Tom *slits his own wrist in one clean swipe of the knife. The cut is* *just a surface cut, but the effect is dramatic. He never even flinches. When he's done, he drops the knife to the floor.*

Richard Jesus Christ, what the *hell* do you think you're doing –

Richard *goes to* **Tom**, *tries to take hold of* **Tom**'s *injured hand. But* **Tom** *grabs hold of both of* **Richard**'s *hands in his own hands. They are face to face.*

Tom See. Your vulnerability has put you exactly where I want you. I could do . . . just about anything now. Break your arms. Slit your throat.

Richard You're bleeding. Not me.

Tom But I don't notice the blood. You do. There's the difference between us.

There is a moment when **Tom** *might do anything, a single second, perhaps. And then it's gone.* **Tom** *releases* **Richard**'s *hands and steps back. He coolly removes a handkerchief and wraps it around his wrist, while* **Richard** *considers what his friend has done.*

Richard I'll take you to the hospital.

Tom A hankie will do.

Richard I better see if Marge is all right.

Tom She's fine.

Richard I'll be back before midnight.

Tom It's no concern of mine.

Richard I know. I'm just saying –

Tom I know what you're saying.

An awkward silence.

Richard Hey. What if I bring back a couple of Morelli's pizzas on the way home and we could –

Tom I like to eat early.

Richard Look, Tom. I don't know what to say, what to think.

Tom   I won't wait up.

Tom *exits.*

Richard   Oh come on – not you too. Tom. TOM.

Tom *re-enters with a suitcase.*

Tom   Morelli will have a comfortable room for me. I won't need it for more than two or three weeks.

Richard   Please don't leave.

Tom   I'm in the way. I'm not the kind of person who likes coming between others. I'm not insensitive. I know when I'm not wanted.

Richard   You're wanted.

Tom   Marge doesn't want me. Marge would like me as far away from you as possible.

Richard   Jeez, hold on. Marge isn't – anyway, you make it sound like she's, I don't know, jealous or something, like you and me, we're involved in some kind of . . . hey. Don't mind me. I'm babbling. I had a couple too many Chiantis at lunch. I don't know what I'm saying.

Tom   Don't you?

Richard   I think we should ask Marge along to Greece.

Tom   I don't.

Richard   I think she wants to be included, you know, in trips and lunch and stupid stuff like that.

Tom   Our trips are stupid?

Richard   No, no. That's not what I – (*Beat.*) Okay. Listen. Maybe you're right. You should go. Leave us alone for a while. I mean, you'll just be up the hill. At the Miramare.

A silence.

Tom All right. (*Pause.*) Fine. (*Pause.*) I'll book a room this evening. You've made your point.

Tom *turns his back on* **Richard**.

Richard Tom. (*Gets no response.*) TOM.

Richard *waits a moment for* **Tom** *to say something.* **Marge** *enters. She wears a bathrobe and fluffy slippers. Her hair is wet. She's just taken a bath. She carries a box of hair-rollers. She sits down at the table and begins to roll her hair, which she will continue to do throughout the scene.*

Marge I'm mortified.

Tom (*with his back to* **Richard**) I'm disappointed.

Richard I'm confused. I don't know what I've done to – I guess there's nothing more to be said, (*Beat.*) See you around, Tom.

Richard *enters* **Marge**'s *scene.* **Tom** *kneels, opens the suitcase, begins unpacking clothes. They are all very neatly folded – shirts, trousers, jackets. He unfolds the clothes fully, lays them out carefully on the floor as if there's a person wearing them – arms and legs outstretched.*

Marge I think I have a pretty firm grasp on my emotions. I'm tough. At least, I thought I was. Now. Well, I promise you I could have picked up a knife. I could have used it. I stood in that room and I thought, please God give me the strength. Give me the *will*. I had the desire.

Richard Do you think I should have asked him to leave?

Marge I feel terrible about all this.

Richard I was a bit hard on him, wasn't I? I mean, he's not to blame for our problems.

Marge Of course he's not. (*Beat.*) Do you think we have problems? A few hours ago you wouldn't even admit to our having a relationship.

Richard Yeah. Well. I'm sorry.

Tom *begins to remove all of his clothes. He dumps his own clothes into the suitcase. When he's finished, he dresses with clothes from the items he's laid out on the floor.*

Tom (*imitating* **Richard**, *but out to us rather than to* **Richard** *and* **Marge**) Yeah. Well. I'm sorry.

Marge What are you sorry about? Insulting our relationship or the fact that we *have* one?

Richard You know what I mean. It's just –

Tom You know what I mean. It's just –

Richard I have a hard time talking. About things. Like this. In front of. People.

Tom I have a hard time talking. About things. Like this. (*As himself.*) HE HAS A HARD TIME. SO WHAT. SOWHATSOWHATSOWHAT.

Marge So? It's not a crime. (*Beat.*) You know, I picked Mongibello at random when I came to Italy. Flat broke and no prospects. Who knew what to expect. And there you were, on the pier, with your big feet and your funny smile. Pulling in a boat for a stranger. Your ease. Your unguarded generosity. I was overwhelmed. Can you blame me for convincing myself I could never leave?

Richard Never say never.

Tom We have problems.

Marge I believe in absolutes.

Tom Her absolute sentimentality, for one thing. What's *wrong* with him? What kind of a man indulges this . . . this . . . *revolting* romantic excess? What he *ought* to do is, he ought to grab the bitch, slap her around a few times and then we'd see – then we'd – we'd see what *she* was made of.

Richard *comes up behind* **Marge** *and gently places his arms around her.*

Richard I don't ask for your devotion, Marge. But I sure do like it.

Marge (*continues with her rollers*)   I know that. I give devotion. Freely. I'm a devoted sort of gal.

Richard   That means the world to me.

Tom   And when he's put her in her place, he's got to say: now look here, Marge. I haven't got time for your hearts and flowers and GODDAMNED KITTENS. I've got to put your feelings aside for once and think about MY OWN PLEASURE.

Tom *stands up, triumphant. He's wearing exactly what* **Richard***'s wearing.*

Richard   I know I haven't made a lot of time for you lately. I know I've been selfish. And I know I've let Tom dictate, well, pretty much the course my days take. But the truth is, I wander. Lose myself. Always have and always will. Usually I find somebody to spin me around, point me in the right direction and send me on my way.

Marge   I thought I did that for you.

Richard   You did. You do. But sometimes . . . well, you can take more than one direction is all I'm saying.

Tom   All I'm saying is, I NEED MY PLEASURE MARGE. And Tom pleases me. He's a sensitive man. But also tough and fair and able to withstand his fair share of PAIN. Men understand pain. Men understand each other's pain. There is an unspoken – a noble – an *understanding* among men. And this understanding is utterly pure. Utterly without . . . emotional complication. I'm sorry Marge, but if you force me to choose, I will NEVER CHOOSE YOU.

Marge   You can't walk in two directions at once. It's physically impossible.

Richard   Are you asking me to choose, Marge? Because if you are, you know I'll always choose you.

Marge   But you know I'd never ask.

Richard So. What's the problem?

Tom What's the *problem?* He wants to know what the PROBLEM is?

Marge The problem is: you haven't kissed me in weeks.

Tom The problem is: the thought of kissing you, Marge, the thought of my lips coming within an inch of your quivering, gaping hole of a MOUTH makes me want to VOMIT.

Richard Well. I can solve that problem.

Richard *turns her towards him. He takes a roller out of her hand.*

Marge I guess I don't look too alluring at the moment.

Tom Guess what, Marge: YOU NEVER DO.

Richard You look . . . swell.

Marge (*laughs*) You really don't have a feel for words. But it's sweet. Endearing.

Tom Stop. Stop now. Stop there.

Richard I may not have a way with words, but I *do* know how to use my mouth.

Marge Show me.

Tom No. Nein. Non. Absolutely not. No no no. NO.

Richard *kisses* **Marge**. *It's a long, slow, passionate kiss.*

Tom The thing is, I can't be everywhere at once. I have myself to blame. I waste time. Now. I'm wasting time. But I can't help the way I look in his clothes. I can't help that they suit me more than they suit him. Look at the cut of this jacket. See? He's a little too broad in the beam for it. Oh, yes. Yes yes yes – too much of Marge's pasta piles on the pounds. See? But on me – on *me* – I was born to wear this jacket. And these trousers. *I* can button them. *He* can't. She's had to sew on an extra button. An *extra button*. I'm sorry. These trousers are not meant to be worn that way. The material is simply too fine for it. Oh, yes. Yes yes yes.

I *fill* these shoes. I am. Entitled.

Richard *and* **Marge** *have not broken their embrace.* **Richard** *picks* **Marge** *up in his arms and carries her off. The sound of the motorboat begins – distant and almost unidentifiable.*

Herbert *enters. He smokes a pipe.*

Herbert   Dear Tom. Stop. No word from you in over five weeks. Stop. We assume the worst. Stop. Thank you for your efforts. Stop. Your outward boat leaves Southampton ten January. Stop. Regards. Stop.

The sound of the motorboat is closer, faster. **Tom** *takes a raincoat from the suitcase and puts it on.* **Herbert** *exits as* **Emily** *enters. She wears a lovely wig.*

Emily   Dear Tom. It breaks my heart not to have news of Richard. Can he be so callous? Can you have failed so miserably? I am no better, but I'm not any worse. Though in an effort to keep myself amused I *have* purchased several wigs. I find I'm partial to ash blonde. Please don't bother to visit on your return. I'm sure you understand the difficulties. With all best wishes.

The sound of the motorboat picks up speed, intensifies. **Emily** *exits as* **Marc** *enters. He's all bundled up against the cold.*

Marc   Tommy. You wouldn't *believe* the frost. Frozen stiff before *Thanksgiving*. The pipes have all burst and my new neighbour wears a black velvet cape and lurks. Late at night. In the hallway. Outside my door. Do you think I should invite him *inside*? Anyhow. Would you mind terribly dropping my brawny detective friend a line? He phoned – ever so politely – the other night just to say you are the *only* resident of chez tenement he hasn't *interrogated* about this George McAlpin business and he'd *really* like to have *your* statement. Who knew you'd ever be so important? Yours ever sincerely truly and blah blah blah.

He exists as **Aunt Dottie** *enters.* **Tom** *begins to hyperventilate.*

Aunt Dottie   Tom. How *dare* you write to the bank without my knowledge. It's a good thing Henry Foster is a

dear friend and valued manager else I'd never have
realized what you were up to. Really, Tom. What were you
thinking when you suggested I might no longer be capable of
making my own financial decisions? Thank goodness you've
only managed to cheat me out of one month's allowance.
You will say thirty dollars is not a lot to cry about, but I'm
afraid Mr Foster and a couple of discreet bank detectives
will be meeting you at the pier upon your return.
Regretfully and with bitter disappointment, I remain.

She exits. The motorboat sound is now unbearably close and fast and
violent.

Tom   STOP. THIS IS NOT THE DREAM. THIS IS
NOT – NOT – MAKE IT – STOP IT – PUSH IT – I
WON'T GO BACK I CAN'T GO BACK I MUSTN'T
GO I WITHER I SHRINK I – NEVER NEVER. NO.

And suddenly, it is calm. The sound of gulls. Gentle waves. Peace.
Stillness. **Tom** *takes a few deep breaths. He's calming down. He's*
calm. **Fausto** *runs on.*

Fausto   Signor Tom – accident. Flood. Thunder.
Collapse. Fausto no explain.

Tom   Calm down. Tell me what's happened.

Fausto   Flash storm. Diluvio. Very dangerous. Signor
Morelli, lucky to escape.

Tom   Has there been a storm?

Fausto   Si, si. Terrible. Signor Tom no *hear*? The
Miramare, the roof. It blow away. Boom. Gone. Collapsed
in storm. (*Beat.*) Fausto can have cigarette now?

Tom *fishes out a cigarette for* **Fausto**. *He places the cigarette*
between **Fausto**'s *lips and lights it for him.* **Fausto** *inhales deeply.*

Tom   I enjoy watching you smoke, Fausto. You take such
pleasure in it.

Richard *and* **Marge** *enter. They hold hands.*

Richard   Three days in Rome. One in San Remo. He

sees the sights, I put him on train, he's gone. It's not much
to ask.

Marge   I didn't say it was. (*Beat.*) I guess we have been
pretty inhospitable to Tom these last few weeks. Me,
especially.

Richard   I'm sure Rome will go a long way towards
putting things right between us.

Marge   Have a good time. I guess. Though I don't like
to think you *can* have a good time without me.

Fausto   Signor Tom stay in Mongibello. Fausto like his
American cigarettes.

Tom   Signor Tom doesn't like to put down roots. Signor
Tom needs to keep moving.

Fausto   But it's nice to stay still in the sunshine, no?

Tom   I have a delicate skin, Fausto. Here.

Tom *gives* **Fausto** *an entire pack of cigarettes.*

Fausto   Lucky Strike. Stupendo.

Marge   Bring me back some perfume from that shop near
the Colosseum. It's called –

Richard   I know, I know – Stradivari.

Marge   You remember. I'm touched.

Richard   See? I'm not a total loss.

Tom   Think of me sometime.

Fausto   Si. Fausto smoke the Lucky cigarettes and think
good thoughts. He think: Signor Tom. (*Beat.*) Hey. See
Fausto do this – for the old time sake.

Fausto *runs off with* **Tom**'s *suitcase.* **Tom** *smiles.*

Marge   And it wouldn't kill you to send me a postcard.
Wish you were here the weather's lousy will suffice.

Richard   Gee. Don't know if I can handle that much

script on one postcard. But for you – I'll do my best. (*Beat.*) See you around, Marge.

Richard *leans down to kiss her.* **Marge** *puts her arms around his neck.*

Marge   Rickie, I really. That is, I want to tell you – how can I say – this is so *silly*, but I can't seem to get the words out. Okay. Here goes. Richard. I think I've fallen madly, wildly, ridiculously in –

Richard *touches two fingers to* **Marge***'s lips.*

Richard   Ssssh. Save it for the postcards.

They smile. They kiss.

Tom   And so. The dream begins.

Marge *exits, waving goodbye.* **Tom** *enters* **Richard***'s scene.* **Tom** *removes a pint bottle of whisky from his raincoat. He drinks. He passes the bottle to* **Richard***.* **Richard** *drinks. They pass the bottle back and forth.*

Richard   There's never a taxi in Rome when you need one. Lotta hills, no taxis.

Tom   I don't mind. It's a pleasant night.

Richard   No stars. I hate nights without stars.

Tom   I love clear night skies. Reminds me of being a kid in Springfield. Missouri's great for black sky.

Richard   Texas.

Tom   Hmmm?

Richard   San Antonio. You come from Texas. Not Missouri.

Tom   That's right.

Richard   So what's with the Ozark skies?

A silence.

Tom   We had relatives. In Springfield. My father's

brother was a machinist.

Richard I guess your daddy was the black sheep. Being a diplomat.

Tom He *owned* several machine shops. My uncle.

Richard Hey – there's a taxi. TAXI. HEY TAXI. You'd think we were invisible.

Tom What if we were?

Richard Who knows. It's not possible, anyway. So why waste your time supposing.

Tom But what if we *were* invisible? What if, unseen, we could partake in any behaviour, however questionable, and never be held accountable for our actions?

Richard There's always a reckoning. Sooner or later somebody's gonna tally the accounts.

Tom But who's going to be held responsible? If nobody sees anything happen?

Richard Just because a thing isn't seen doesn't mean it's not there.

Tom That's where you're wrong. We can't identify things we can't see. Things we can't touch or smell or taste.

Richard Yeah, well, I can't really taste this booze anymore but I betcha it's going into my tummy all the same. Taxi!

Sophia *enters. She is a magnificent creation, all breasts, eyelashes and curls.*

Sophia What's your hurry boys?

Tom Go away. We're invisible.

Richard *and* **Tom** *laugh.*

Sophia I'm sure you are, darling. But Sophia sees you all the same. It's my curse.

Tom Lucky us.

Richard   Sophia. Ah. Beautiful name. Like Loren.

Sophia   No, no. Like the *city*. It has many twists and turns and so do I.

Richard *and* **Sophia** *laugh.*

Richard   Would you like a drink, Sophia? Our mouths are clean. Cross our hearts.

Sophia   Sophia doesn't drink. But Sophia *is* hungry.

Tom   Imagine that.

Sophia   You know, I think I hear an annoying little buzz of a voice somewhere. Somewhere far off. But I can't be sure. Because it is an *invisible* voice.

Sophia *and* **Richard** *laugh again.* **Richard** *approaches* **Sophia**. *He holds out the whisky bottle to her.*

Richard   Here, Sophia. This is veal piccata from the finest kitchen in all of Rome.

Sophia   Thank you, darling. Don't mind if I do.

Sophia *takes the bottle. She drinks deeply. She holds it out to* **Tom**.

Tom   No. Thank you.

Sophia   Suit yourself. Uh-oh. What a shame. All gone.

She drinks again. She gives the bottle back to **Richard**. *It's empty.* **Richard** *laughs.* **Sophia** *laughs.*

Sophia   But you know, Sophia is *still* hungry.

Richard   Well, uh, just how much is it gonna cost a fella to feed Sophia?

Sophia   Let's eat first, talk business later.

Sophia *grabs* **Richard** *by his lapels and kisses him.*

Richard   Wow. Talk about being taken by surprise.

Sophia *and* **Richard** *laugh.*

Richard   Let me see if I was imagining it.

He kisses her.

Richard   Either you are pure dynamite or I have one very vivid imagination.

Sophia   Or . . . I could be invisible.

Sophia *and* **Richard** *laugh.*

Tom   There are no taxis in this road. We'll have to move on.

Sophia   Not so fast.

Richard   I sense a proposition floating its way to *you*, Tom.

Sophia *and* **Richard** *laugh.* **Sophia***, keeping hold of* **Richard** *with one hand, pulls* **Tom** *to her with her other hand. She is sandwiched between the two men.*

Sophia   So tense. Loosen up, bambino. Nothing to fear with Sophia. We share.

Tom   What? What do we *share*? What are you talking about?

Sophia   This.

Sophia *kisses* **Tom** *deeply. He resists at first, then gives in to it. She pulls away. She kisses* **Richard**. *She enjoys it.* **Tom** *pulls her back towards him. He kisses her. He bites her.*

Sophia   Ouch. Easy, darling. Easy does it.

Richard   (*laughs*)   Those still waters sure do run deep, Tom.

Tom *puts his arms around* **Sophia***'s waist so that his hands almost touch* **Richard***'s hands.* **Tom** *kisses* **Sophia**. *While embracing* **Tom***,* **Sophia** *pulls his arms closer around her body.* **Richard** *begins to kiss her neck. He runs his hands up her thighs, up her dress.* **Sophia** *breaks away from them.*

Sophia   Naughty boy. No touching under Sophia's clothes.

Richard *laughs*.

Tom   Why not. You asked us. You started it. Finish it.

Sophia   I start nothing I don't intend to finish. But this is not my way.

Tom   Slut.

Richard   Hey now, Tom. There's no need for −

Tom   A tease. That's all she is. Like Marge.

Richard   Okay. That's enough.

Sophia (*to* **Richard**)   I like you. I thought we were having a good time. Sophia likes good times. But him − I think you better do yourself a favour and lose him in a tourist trap.

Tom   You think I'm a *tourist*? You common whore.

Tom *pushes* **Sophia** *down to the ground. He kneels beside her, pins her down.*

Richard   Tom − TOM. That's enough. You've gone too far. Leave her be.

Sophia   That's right. Leave Sophia be and Sophia will forget she ever saw you.

Tom   You want money, don't you? You were going to take our *money*.

Sophia   I don't need your money. I have money.

Richard   Nobody said anything about money. Come on, Tom. Let me help you up.

Richard *goes to help* **Tom** *away from* **Sophia**. **Tom** *pushes him away*. **Richard** *staggers backwards, falls*.

Tom   Rape her. Come on. I'll hold her down.

Richard   Tom. You don't know what you're saying.

Sophia   Giù le mani. LASCIA. (*To* **Richard**.) Chiami la polizia. Presto.

Tom   There's no point in calling the police, Sophia. They take no notice of whores. Come on, Richard. We're invisible. We're not responsible.

A pause. **Richard** *approaches* **Sophia**. *He unbuckles his belt.*

Tom   That's right. I'll watch you. It'll be fine.

Sophia (*to* **Richard**)   He's crazy, Don't let him push you into this. You're not like him. DO NOT DO THIS.

Freddie Miles *enters. He's dressed in black tie.* **Richard** *hurriedly buckles up.* **Tom** *sees* **Freddie** *and without missing a beat nonchalantly eases off of* **Sophia**.

Tom   You're not worth what you cost. Go on. Get out of here.

Tom *removes a fat roll of lire from his raincoat pocket and puts it on the ground in front of* **Sophia**. *He gets up, dusts himself down, lights a cigarette.* **Sophia** *stares at the money.*

Freddie   Che cosa c'e, signorina?

Sophia   No problem. I am just leaving.

Sophia *collects the money. She starts to get up.* **Richard** *bends to help her. She shrugs off his help.*

Freddie   Are you sure you're all right? I'm happy to escort you to a taxi or –

Tom   She's all right.

Freddie   I'd rather hear it from the lady, if you don't mind.

Sophia   I am fine. I go now. This ... this never *touch* me.

Sophia *approaches* **Tom**. *She comes very close to him, spits in his face. A pause, before he turns away from her.* **Sophia** *throws down the money and exits.* **Tom** *cleans himself of* **Sophia**'s *spittle.* **Richard** *collects the money.*

Freddie   I've gotta tell ya, buddy. I don't like what I saw.

Richard   Forget it. A misunderstanding.

Freddie   Guy had his hands around her throat. That's some misunderstanding.

Richard   Look. It's not what it seems. We booked her for the night. My friend here had a few too many. He couldn't . . . well, he couldn't hold up his end of the bargain. And you know how Italian women are. Let's just say she was kinda vocal in her disapproval. They argued, it got out of hand, he was a little rough, but . . . there was no harm in the end. He offered her good money. You saw that.

Richard *gets up, goes to* **Freddie**, *offers a handshake.*

Freddie   Hey – I'll be damned. If it isn't Rickie Greenleaf. Well I'll be a monkey's – of all the people to come across –

Freddie *grabs* **Richard**'s *hand, shakes it vigorously.*

Richard   Freddie? Freddie *Miles*? Sonofabitch.

Tom (*to the audience*)   And just when you least expect a crisis, the biggest one hits you square in the face, a big Fat Freddie Miles fastball over the plate. The goalie hits a home run.

Freddie   Sweet Jesus, buddy, it's been –

Richard   – ages. Centuries. But, hey, it's great to *see* you and by the looks of it you're doing pretty damn okay –

Freddie   – but how in the hell have you been *keeping* yourself? Christ, you look terrific. I got business in Milan and figured a guy ain't worth his salt if he doesn't see Rome before he dies so, what the heck, I toss on this monkey suit and here I am. Lemme *look* at you.

Richard *steps back, holding his arms out to his sides.*

Richard   Here I am. Jeez, Freddie – this is just – well, hold on now – you know Tom. Tom Ripley. Come here, Tom. You remember Freddie from the old days, don't you?

Tom   Of course I do. Hello, Freddie. Been a long time.

Tom *shakes* **Freddie***'s hand.*

Freddie   I guess it must be 'cause I sure don't remember you.

Richard   Tom was your back-up goalie. At Choate. Remember that time I beat the –

Tom *(interrupts)*   I was a couple of years behind you. Transfer from a southern prep.

Freddie   Yeah? Which one? I hail from Winston Salem, myself. If you're a good ole boy, I'll place you.

Tom   Clarkeville Hall. Small prep outside of San Antonio.

Freddie   Huh. Can't say I know it. But I guess Texas ain't exactly my part of the world. *(Beat.)* Sorry buddy, but I don't recall you at all.

Tom   I've always been nondescript. I don't mind.

Richard *(puts an arm around* **Freddie***'s shoulder)*   Whaddya say we find us an after-hours joint? We got tons of catching up to do before me and Tom head down to San Remo in the morning. I still can't believe my eyes. Freddie *Miles*. I'll be *damned*.

Richard *and* **Freddie** *wander off into the night. The sound of the waves, the gulls, the gentle sea, is heard.*

Tom   The truth is, I should have seen this coming. The world is too small. Freddie Miles is unavoidable. Freddie Miles is everywhere. And if it's not Freddie, then it's another imbecilic school chum. Lurking in the Sistine Chapel. Loitering in the Piazza San Marco. Missing a train in Florence and stumbling upon us in some ghastly trattoria. And *him*. How dare he indulge in smug nostalgic drinking binges with men whose names and faces he barely remembers. Freddie Miles. And *how* could he confuse me with that, that *gargantua*? Let's face it, Rickie doesn't suit himself. He's not made for his lifestyle. He doesn't *fit* into the life he leads with any comfort. He can't paint. His talent is laughable. I don't even *wish* to paint and yet – my copies of his watercolours are far better, have far more subtlety than his originals. I'm sure I'm better with his parents. I'm sure Mrs Greenleaf wishes I could have been her son. In fact, Rickie has no *aptitude* for any part of the life he leads. Except, of course, for Marge. And he's welcome to that particular aptitude. Now me, I'll take the rest of it. I will. Make no mistake. I have all the talent in this family.

Richard *enters. He carries a picnic basket and two oars under one arm.*

Richard   Motorboats are great. Unless you just want to drift.

Tom   Drifting makes me nervous.

Richard   Drifting's relaxing. Anyway, that's why I've brought these along. (*Refers to the oars.*) We'll make our way out for about a mile, then . . . we'll cut the motor and drift. Here's lunch.

Richard *hands* **Tom** *the picnic basket. He opens it, pulls out a bottle of perfume.*

Tom   What's this?

Richard   *That's* where I put it. Stradivari. (**Tom** *hasn't a clue.*) Perfume. For Marge. Her favourite. Let's go.

Richard *takes the perfume. They sit down. The sound of the motorboat begins. It gradually overwhelms the gentle sea sounds.*

Tom   I might get seasick.

Richard   Has it ever happened to you before?

Tom   No. But it might.

Richard (*laughs*)   You can be such an old lady sometimes, Tom.

Tom   What does that mean?

Richard   Nothing. It's just –

Tom   Do you mean that sometimes I behave like a
woman?

Richard   God, no, it's just an expression. I mean, Marge
says you can get pretty picky, and when you get picky your
mouth crinkles up in a tight little smile. Like her
grandmother.

Tom   Marge ought to mind her own business. (*Beat.*) I'm
sorry. I shouldn't have said that. I apologise.

Richard   Listen, forget it. I have.

Silence, save for the sound of the motorboat.

Tom   It's certainly monotonous out here.

Richard   I don't know. Once you get to know the sea
you realize it never makes itself completely known. It
always holds something back.

Tom   Like Sophia.

Richard   Well. No. That's not what I meant.

Tom   Oh.

More silence.

Richard   We haven't said much about Sophia.

Tom   Should we say much about her?

Richard   It's – we were –

Tom   We were drunk.

Richard   I was drunk.

Tom   Like you told Freddie. We hired her. I was drunk. I
couldn't perform. I was a little rude. End of story.

Richard   I invented that story.

Tom   Did you?

Richard   For Chrissake, Tom. Of course I did. What was
I going to tell Freddie? Huh? Oh, sure, we almost *raped* a
girl and Tom probably would have *strangled* her if you
hadn't come along?

Tom   We were drunk. You said so. And in saying so, you made it *fact*. The rest is unimportant. What's done is done.

More silence.

Richard   What will you do when you get back?

Tom   I expect there's a dealer or two in Milan I should phone for –

Richard (*interrupts*)   I meant when you get home. To New York.

Tom (*after a moment*)   New York. Yes.

Richard   Look, I know it's not your area or anything, and if it's a problem just say so, but I thought as long as you're going, you might as well take a few of my paintings with you.

Tom   You don't have to give me gifts, Rickie.

Richard (*laughs*)   Hell, no. I was thinking you could sell them for me. I mean, of course I'd pay you a commission. Whatever you want.

Tom   Whatever I want?

Richard   It's just – well, Marge thinks people would snap 'em up. Watercolours are big, she says. And it's about time I started thinking about my future.

Tom   Why ruin the present by worrying about the future?

Richard   You can't stand still waiting for life to take you by surprise. You've got to make plans. (*Beat.*) Anyway, will you take the paintings?

More silence.

Tom   What if I said I wasn't going back to New York.

Richard   But you are going back.

Tom   But what if I said I wasn't.

Richard   You've made your plans already, Tom.

Tom   I never plan. It lacks . . . imagination. So. If I said I wasn't going back to New York. If I said I would stay. With you. What then?

Richard *hesitates before speaking.*

Richard   I'm gonna propose to Marge.

Tom   Oh.

Richard   I don't know, it just occurred to me and, well, I'm not getting any younger.

Tom   Yes.

Richard   All right, you could be a *little* enthusiastic for me, buddy.

Tom   Of course. Congratulations. I'm sure she'll be very happy.

Richard   Why put off the inevitable? I think Marge and me, we've been headed this way for some time. We have this joke, Marge and me, that we'll live happily ever after like they do in stories, only we'll do it mostly under cover. Get it? (**Tom** *doesn't.*) You know, under-the-sheets, under cover . . . well. It's not important. In a way, I have you to thank for opening my eyes.

Tom   Really.

Richard   Yeah. I mean, you've made me think long and hard about the choices I've made. Who knows. Maybe I'll even learn to like my dad and his shipyard. Maybe Marge and my mom will become bridge partners.

The motorboat sounds stop. Stillness. The sound of the boat rocking on the waves.

Richard   Right. This is as good a place as any. Now, if you feel the boat drift in a direction you don't like, just take one of these and – (*He demonstrates with an oar.*) push it around a little like this and . . . there you go. Right as rain. Okay. Let's chow down.

Richard *opens the picnic basket and greedily attacks a couple of* *sandwiches.* **Tom** *watches him eat. He is very still.*

Tom   Do you trust me, Rickie?

Richard   Hey, sure, you're a pal.

Tom   You'd tell me things you wouldn't tell Marge. For instance. You trust me that much.

Richard   Well. Marge. That's different. That's – personal. Come on, Tom. Friends are one thing, but Marge, that's . . . you know what I mean.

Tom   Yes. I'm sorry to say I do. (*Beat; he watches* **Richard** *devour the sandwiches.*) I doubt very much whether your mother and Marge will become bosom pals.

Richard (*with his mouth full of food*)   Why not?

Tom   Because your mother is dying. (*Beat.*) You really shouldn't talk with your mouth full. It's disgusting.

Richard   What did you say? Would you – repeat what you just said.

Tom   Certainly. Your mother is dying. A terrible cancer. Quite inoperable.

Richard   How do you know – how is it *possible* that you know – my *mother* is dying?

Tom   Your father's given up on you, so I wouldn't bother harbouring any residual feelings about the family business. He's probably going to find a cousin or a nephew to train up. Or a total stranger. He hardly pays attention to your mother anymore. It's very sad.

Richard   Look, Tom. I don't know what kind of a sick joke you think this is, but I haven't seen you in years. Not since school. You haven't seen my family in *years*. You don't know a thing about us.

Tom   Oh. And before I forget to mention it: I don't even know *you*. I've met you once. At a wedding. You were plastered. I was drawn to you. I didn't know why then, but I know now. It's funny how you – your family – all of you were so eager to *know* me. I'd say it's fate. But I don't believe in all that, do you?

Richard   Why you arrogant little bastard, I could tear you to pieces I could –

Tom   Please, no histrionics. If only your pathetic watercolours harboured that kind of energy. Now. Watch me.

Tom *stands up, removes his raincoat. He is, of course, dressed identically to* **Richard**. *He sits down. He's beaming.*

Tom   How do you like the new me?

Richard   Those are *my* clothes.

Tom   They fit me ever so much better than they fit you.

Richard   That's it. I'm gonna break your goddamned NECK YOU BASTARD YOU –

Richard *stands up and lunges for* **Tom**. *The sound of the motorboat comes in suddenly and very violently, as if* **Tom** *has quite instinctively switched it on at the highest speed.* **Richard** *falls down and backwards, as if he's fallen partially out of the boat. He fights the motion of the boat and the water in order to hang on to the edge of the boat with his fingers.* **Tom** *does nothing to help him.*

Richard   TOM – TOM – TAKE MY HAND – PLEASEPLEASEPLEASE –

Tom *bends towards* **Richard** *as if to take his hand.* **Richard** *reaches out one hand to* **Tom**. *The sound of the waves and the motorboat are increasingly unstable and violent.* **Tom** *reaches out his hand towards* **Richard**, *their fingers almost touch, and at the last possible moment,* **Tom** *raises an oar and brings it down viciously on to* **Richard***'s head. He beats him again. And again. But* **Richard** *manages somehow to grab hold of the oar and with a last incredible display of strength, he pulls* **Tom** *out of the boat. They both disappear underneath the waves. The sounds of the motorboat and the unstable sea become deafening for an instant and then – a sudden startling silence.*

Blackout.

Act Two

Darkness. The sound of running water. A slight trickle, then a gentle and steady stream, building to a roar – white water, a waterfall. It's deafening for a moment, then abrupt silence as the lights come up on **Tom**. *He wears a pristine white robe. He's barefoot. His hair is wet. He stands in front of a full-length mirror. He looks into the mirror as he uses a small comb to part and re-part his hair. He rehearses speaking to* **Marge** *as* **Richard** *would.*

Tom Hello Marge. Hello *Marge*. Ciao Marge. No. That's not it. (*Beat.*) Good morning, Marge. It's Rickie. Hi Marge. It's *Richard*. Hello. It's me. It is I. It's – no no no. That's not. *It*. That's not – the part is just slightly – ever so slightly – ever so slightly – not. *It*.

He steps back from the mirror. He turns, in profile, checks out that particular view of himself in the mirror.

Tom Look Marge, let's face facts. I'm not coming back. I'm bored with Mongibello and I'm finished with you. (*Beat.*) I'm so sorry. I'm awfully sorry, Marge. But I must be frank. I don't love you. The truth is, I *can't* love you because I love – I *can't* live with you because I'm living with – It's very simple. Tom and I are travelling together. The world is our – No no *no*. I have to get it *right*.

Tom *re-parts his hair very carefully and precisely. He steps right up to the mirror and tenderly touches the reflection of his face.*

Tom I don't want to hurt you, Marge. Let's part on good terms. I want that more than anything. Tom wants it. Don't cry. Please. I can't bear sadness. It's undignified.

Tom *takes hold of the mirror with both hands as if he's taking hold of* **Marge**. *He leans in to kiss the mirror as if to kiss* **Marge**. *He stops just short of kissing the mirror.*

Tom No last kiss? Well. Whatever you want, Marge. Tom said you'd be strong.

Tom *steps back, examines himself once more in the mirror. He adjusts his hair's parting slightly. He tucks the comb into one of his pockets.*

Tom   Perfection.

Tom *removes a tube of lipstick from his pocket. He opens the lipstick, sniffs, it, dabs a bit onto the back of his hand.*

Tom   Sorry I lifted your lipstick, Marge. But it was never really *you*. It's far too subtle a colour. Look at it this way. I've saved you from further public embarrassment.

Tom *steps up to the mirror and begins writing on its surface with the lipstick. He forges* **Richard**'*s signature over and over again. Throughout all of this,* **Tom** *speaks:*

Tom   The boat was problematic, Rickie. But its disposal did take my mind off the horror of the *water*. So I do have one thing to thank you for. I didn't think I'd ever learn to swim.

Tom *steps back from the mirror to examine his work. He rubs out a bit of one signature, sets about correcting it.*

Tom   Perfection. (*Beat.*) The dream transforms. As I watch the boat sink deep the dream becomes Mykonos. You and I. A fluid heat. Slow-moving shirtless boys, our reluctant bellhops. Their heavy-lidded eyes and thick fingers. Their constant backward glances. There's no escaping them. And salt. Salt everywhere. Ancient pillars of the stuff, rising from the water. And there we are, you and I. Waving to each other from the tops of two salt mountains. You hold out a piece of toast to me. You say –

Richard *enters. He wears a pristine white robe. He's barefoot. His hair is wet. He eats some toast.*

Richard   Hey, Tom. You want some toast? It burned a hell of a hole through the pier, but fortunately the bread's okay.

Tom   – want some toast, Tom? (*Beat.*) I'm suddenly very hungry. I lean across my salt mountain towards what you offer. I'm almost there. I'm touching your fingertips. I can hardly believe my luck and then you speak the unspeakable.

Richard   Where's Marge? Did we leave her on the pier?

Tom   Did we leave her on the *pier*? Have you lost your *mind*? The snakes got Marge. The sea got Marge. I stole her lipstick, the pier collapsed and the tide flushed Marge *away*. Don't you remember?

Richard (*munching on the toast*)   Oh, sure. I remember.

Tom *resumes forging* **Richard**'s *signature*. **Richard** *steps up to see how* **Tom**'s *getting on. They stand side by side.* **Richard** *finishes the toast as he watches* **Tom** *forge his signature.*

Richard   The 'G' isn't quite right.

Tom   What? What's wrong? The loop? Oh no no – I see. The *slant*. Too much to the right.

Richard   Too *little* to the right. Here. Let me show you.

Richard *comes up behind* **Tom**, *takes* **Tom**'s *writing hand into his own hand and guides them both in a signature over the mirror.*

Richard   See. There's no break from the 'G' to the 'R'. And then . . . wait a minute – here. Look here. There's a slight break between the 'N' and the 'L' and after that . . .

Tom   I know. The rest of the signature is virtually illegible.

Richard   Eccellente. Again?

And **Richard** *once again guides* **Tom**'s *hand in a signature over the mirror. When they're done, they step back together to admire their work.*

Tom   Perfection.

They turn towards each other. They are very close.

Tom   Tell me now.

Richard   If not for you, life would be meaningless.

Tom No no – not *meaningless*. That's excessive.

Richard Empty. Life would be empty.

Tom Yes. That's better. What else.

Richard I was wrong to question your motives. I see now that Marge was a bad idea.

Tom A *mistake*. Say it.

Richard Marge was a mistake. You were right.

Tom I *am* right. I am always right. And?

Richard You are . . . genius personified.

Tom Wise and witty and worldy and winning.

Richard Because you are me.

Tom Because I am you.

Tom *unties* **Richard***'s robe belt.* **Richard** *unties* **Tom***'s robe belt. Their robes fall open. They wear identical undergarments.*

Tom And this is the happiest moment of my life.

Tom *offers his hand to* **Richard**. **Richard** *is just about to take it when* **Silvio** *enters. As* **Silvio** *speaks,* **Richard** *disappears.*

Silvio Signor Greenleaf is ready to be dressed?

Silvio *carries some clothing.* **Tom** *hastily re-ties his robe.*

Tom No. Signor Greenleaf is not ready to be dressed.

Silvio But you call me. I hear you. From the other room.

Tom You are mistaken.

Silvio My ears are good. I hear what I hear. And I hear *you*. You speak to me. I come. (*Beat.*) You left me alone in the bath. I got cold.

Tom Very well. Signor Greenleaf is ready to be dressed.

Tom *tries to take the clothes from* **Silvio**. **Silvio** *playfully backs away from him.*

Silvio   Maybe Silvio not ready to dress you.

Tom   I'm quite capable of dressing myself.

Silvio   But you pay me so *much*. I think I am the best paid boy in all of Rome. I must do something for all this money, no?

Tom   I pay you to be my valet.

Silvio   What is this word? Valet?

Tom   Well. It's like a . . . manservant.

Silvio   And do these . . . valets . . . bathe their masters?

Tom   Sometimes. Depending. On the master.

Silvio   And do they also bathe *with* their masters?

A silence.

Tom   You may leave the clothes here, Silvio. Thank you.

Silvio *shrugs. He quite pointedly drops* **Tom**'*s clothes on to the floor.*

Silvio   As signor wishes.

A slight pause before **Tom** *begins to gather his clothes and dress.* **Silvio** *doesn't move.*

Tom   Well? Don't stand there like that. What are you waiting for?

Silvio   I watch. I wait. In case.

Tom   In case . . . what?

Marge *enters.*

Marge   In case Rickie phones I'd like to be here. Mongibello's always felt like home to me. To us. He said – well, we said – before he left – we vowed to make a home here together one day. A base. So no matter how far we travelled individually or as a couple there'd always be Mongibello. Waiting. Warm and welcoming and – oh, Tom, did he say *nothing* about why he's left? Is there *no* hope that he'll return?

Silvio In case I am needed. To serve. I am your manservant, no?

Tom I despise literalism. Go on – go. I don't need you today.

Silvio (*refers to the mirror full of lipstick signatures*) Does Signor Greenleaf forget his own name?

Tom *glances at the mirror.*

Tom It's an unflattering mirror. Take it away.

Silvio As signor wishes.

Silvio *begins to wheel the mirror away.*

Marge Three days he said. A short trip to Rome and the coast and then . . . well, Rickie *likes* his routine. Change makes him nervous. He was only just settling into his – the point is, he gave no warning of *this*. Rickie is – *was* – perfectly happy here. At least, as far as I could tell. Perhaps it was some failing on my part that drove him away. What do you think, Tom? Did he say *anything*?

Tom *dresses hastily.* **Silvio** *turns back for a moment. He removes a ring from his pocket, holds it up for* **Tom** *to see.*

Silvio Oh. I almost forget. You left this floating in the bath.

Tom My ring.

Silvio Si. You're lucky it not fall down the drain with the dirty bathwater. You're lucky I rescue it.

Tom Yes. I'm very lucky for many things. Thank you. Now. Give me my ring.

Tom *holds out his upturned palm, waits for* **Silvio** *to give him the ring.* **Silvio** *takes* **Tom**'s *hand instead and slips the ring on to his finger.* **Tom** *eases his hand away from* **Silvio**. **Silvio** *smiles at* **Tom**.

Silvio I always want to do that to somebody. But I never have the chance. You call if you need Silvio. You know the number.

Silvio *exits with the mirror and* **Tom***'s robe.*

Marge   We discuss *everything*. And not just big things, but silly things. You know, like what colour sheets he should buy or whether we should get our wine from Morelli or from a wholesaler. So it's funny he never mentioned this Massini fellow.

Tom *enters the scene with* **Marge**.

Tom   Massimo. He's an important watercolourist and Rickie jumped at the chance to apprentice with him. They'd been corresponding for some time. (*Beat.*) I wasn't aware that you and Rickie bought your wine and sheets together.

Marge   What are you talking about?

Tom   You just said. You discussed everything. Where you should buy your wine. Your sheets.

Marge   We didn't. We don't. I only meant – oh, what's the use. I don't know why Rickie sent you down here to do his dirty work. Tell me directly, Tom. I won't mind.

Tom   Tell you ... what? I've only come so you don't worry about him. He's concerned for you, Marge.

Marge   It doesn't take a genius to figure it out and God knows I'm pretty naïve but I thought I knew him better than this.

Tom   I understand how upsetting Rickie's decision must be for you. No matter what you now believe, he really did – does – care for you a great deal. But in the end, other considerations came first.

Marge   You don't have to sweeten this pill for me, Tom.

Tom   I don't know what you mean, Marge. I'm just the messenger.

Marge   Well. You must think me pretty foolish. I don't

blame you. But it's obvious even to me what's going on. Rickie and I have fun together and I like to think we're good for each other. Okay. I'll be honest, we're not *deliriously* in love, but who is? It's a good, solid fit. And then. You come along. Suddenly, we're not so happy, Rickie and me. We bicker. I'm jealous and petty and defensive. That's not me. That's *never* been me and I don't at all like what I become. I confront Rickie. I give him a ridiculous ultimatum. He panics. He makes me a promise he can't possibly keep. He calms down with some distance from me and sees sense when you two go off to Rome. He sends you down here to set me right. (*Beat.*) He's a coward, I suppose. Can't face the ridicule. Or what he *imagines* would be my ridicule. He clearly doesn't know me as well as I like to think he does. Because I could never reject him. Not even over this. But for heaven's sake, Tom, just *tell* me and put me out of my misery. If you don't say it, I'll always hold out hope.

Tom   Honestly, Marge. You're not making any sense.

Marge   You're both queer. Like I said, it's obvious. (*Beat.*) I'm not angry.

Tom   Oh. I see.

A silence. **Tom** *removes a wrapped package from his jacket pocket and gives it to* **Marge***.*

Tom   Rickie picked this up for you in Rome. No need for repayment. It's a gift. (*Beat.*) Aren't you going to open it?

Marge   So you're just going to ignore this.

Tom   Rickie wants you to have three paintings of your choice. The rest will be put up for sale with the furniture and the house.

Marge   Don't torture me, Tom. If you have any compassion you'll –

Tom (*interrupts her*)   What? Dignify your accusation with a response? Jealousy is one thing, Marge, but hysteria is quite another.

Marge That's not fair.

Tom Isn't it? (*Beat.*) Look. I *do* feel for you. You know as well as I that Rickie is impulsive. But I'm certain he hasn't forgotten you. And he may well be back someday. (*Beat.*) Open your gift. Go on. It'll cheer you up.

Marge *opens the package.*

Marge I know you're right. I *know* there's a good reason for his actions. I trust him. I do. But I wish I understood his impulses a little – (*She's opened the package; it's the perfume.*) – oh for goodness – the Stradivari – he *remembered*. Honestly, Tom, he surprises me so much.

Tom He said it's your favourite.

Marge It is. Every time he goes to Rome I beg him to buy me some. And every time he forgets.

Tom Not this time.

Marge No. Not this time. (*Beat.*) What's different? There's something different about you, Tom.

Tom (*laughs*) Are you speaking metaphorically?

Marge No. No, there's definitely something – have you lost weight?

Tom Well, no. If anything I've *gained* a few pounds. Rickie and I have been eating well. Maybe that's it.

Marge No. It's something else. Your hair, maybe. It's – oh, I don't know. I'm tired. I see things. Don't pay the slightest bit of attention to me. (*Beat.*) Will he write to me sometime, do you think? Or phone?

Tom I think . . . there's a definite possibility. Though, of course, I can't speak for Rickie.

Marge No, no. Of course you can't. I'm sorry. I don't mean to put you on the spot. It's just – I can't abide – I don't – the truth is, I'm careless in my relationships with people. With men. I treat them lightly because, well. Blah blah blah. You know the story. But I swear to you, Tom, I

...man with all my heart. And I will pursue him to ...ds of the earth if I think there is the remotest ...ssibility that he loves me in the same way. I will get down on my knees. I will throw open my arms. I will declare a national holiday. I will ring bells, shout from rooftops, stop traffic, jump for joy, *whatever* it takes. But there has to be the *possibility* for love, for *us*. Please. Please tell me he speaks to you about us. He must do. He trusts you.

Tom I'm sorry, Marge. But he's never mentioned you. In that way.

A pause. **Marge** *opens the perfume, dabs some at her wrists, her neck.*

Marge Do you want some lunch, Tom? Let's see – I've got some fresh tomatoes and basil, two or three different cheeses back at my place. I'm sure Fausto could rustle us up a bit of ham or –

Tom I really ought to be wrapping up here. The trip back to Rome is long and Rickie's expecting me. Besides, I don't want to inconvenience you.

Marge It's no trouble. I like to cook. Keeps me busy. (*Beat.*) I'm sorry, you know, for what I said. That was uncalled for.

Tom Forget it. I have.

Marge No, I mean it. I stepped way over the line and there's no excuse for that. You know, I used to laugh at jealous old women. Now look at me. I feel as if something ugly and small has reached inside me and robbed my heart of all its trust. It's not an attractive quality, is it?

Tom No. But it's . . . understandable. Under the circumstances.

Marge People always say that kind of thing to me: Under the circumstances. Or: We regret to inform you. Or: You win some, you lose some. (*Beat.*) Or maybe it's just you, Tom. Maybe you just make me feel bad.

Tom *rises. He offers a handshake to* **Marge**.

Tom   I'll take a rain check on lunch. Goodbye, Marge.

Marge *does not take his hand,* **Tom** *drops his hand, nods, turns to leave.*

Marge   That ring. It's Rickie's ring.

The slightest of pauses, then:

Tom   Yes. It is.

Marge   He doesn't remove it. Not even for baths.

Tom   I admired it one day. He gave it to me.

Marge   He wouldn't do that.

Tom *turns back to face* **Marge**.

Tom   I think we've just discovered how little you really do know about Rickie. (*Beat.*) Would you please drop the keys at the Miramare when you're done here?

Marge   I always stay in Rickie's house when he's gone.

Tom   But the house is to be sold. And Rickie doesn't want anybody using it. As of today. Of course, I couldn't expect you to have known that. Not being in touch with Rickie. How insensitive of me. I'm sorry.

Marge *holds out the keys to* **Tom**. *He doesn't take them.*

Marge   The Miramare's out of my way. You take them. Tell Rickie I'll wait for him. If that's what he wants. If not . . . well.

Tom   Speaking as a friend, perhaps it might be best if you considered returning to the States.

Marge   Please don't speak as my friend. (*Beat.*) You know, it *is* your hair. New parting, isn't it? Doesn't become you at all.

Marge *tucks the keys into* **Tom**'*s breast pocket and exits.*

Tom (*to the audience*)   She can't touch me. Not at all. A shame. I could teach her a thing or two about cruelty. If she'd let me. The sheer *ease* of it all. Watch her bend first this way, then that. I amaze myself. Throw a dog a bone. Tell her the glass is half full. Show her there's a silver lining to every cloud. Nothing to it. A practice round. But I don't want any more practice. I want to *play*.

Music – festive, light, Italian boulevard music. Accordions and bad percussion. **Silvio** *enters. He's dressed for travel – complete with cameras and cases slung round his neck. They address the following scene, pageant-style – big and bold – to the audience.*

Silvio   Signor Greenleaf's tickets are paid for, his hotels are booked and his trains are running on time. First stop, Perugia.

Tom   Followed by, in quick succession, Siena, Arezzo, Livorno and Pisa. What culture. Photo opportunities abound.

Tom *poses,* **Silvio** *snaps photos.*

Silvio   Two days of rest in Lucca and then . . . Firenze.

Tom   Florence. City of Donatello. One could stay here forever. The colour. The intensity.

Silvio   On the other hand, Signor tires of San Marino almost instantly.

Tom   Of course, Rimini and Ravenna are *much* more my style. Sedate. Reflective. Anticipating invasion. Glorious. (*Beat.*) A month on and our extended holiday is such a success. Onward. Through the hills towards that ultimate destination – Venezia. But first – a minor hitch:

Silvio   Signor's Miracles of the Virgin excursion to Ferrara must be ditched in favour of –

Tom   – cashing the inevitable cheque at Banco Bologna.

Silvio   City of Silvio's birth, Bologna. (*Spots someone in the distance.*) Look – Signor Greenleaf – there she is. Didn't I tell you she'd find me at the station? Ciao, Mama!

Music out. **Silvio** *beams and waves at his unseen mother. He runs off after her.*

Tom (*to the audience*)   Our train pulls in and I can hardly contain my glee, the rush of adrenaline as my nerve anticipates its most crucial test: my hand gripping the pen already poised above the dotted line. I jump from that train, I push through the crowd, I gather speed and run run run down the platform. I race towards this place, this time, this moment of truth.

Richard *enters. He carries a small cashbox. He sits at the table, folds his hands, stares straight ahead.* **Tom** *sits opposite him. He removes a chequebook from his pocket. He writes out a cheque. He's cool, deliberate. He rips out the cheque, slides it over towards* **Richard**, *replaces the chequebook in his pocket.*

Tom   Mi potrebbe dare anche degli spiccioli per favore? The smallest notes you have, grazie.

Richard *picks up the cheque, looks it over.*

Richard   Potrei vedere il suo passaporto?

Tom   My passport. Certainly.

Tom *removes a passport from his pocket, slides it over to* **Richard**. **Richard** *picks it up, opens it, looks from the passport to* **Tom** *to the passport and back again. He closes the passport, puts it down on the table, slides it back to* **Tom**.

Richard   Grazie, Signor Greenleaf.

Tom   You're welcome, Rickie.

Richard   I beg your pardon.

Tom (*he smiles*)   Never mind. Non importa.

Richard   Would you like it all in thousand lire notes, Signor Greenleaf?

Tom   Oh, yes. That would be gorgeous. Thanks.

Richard *opens the cashbox. He counts out an enormous pile of lire. While he does so,* **Tom** *speaks.*

Tom (*to the audience*)   Fate is on my side. Here is the proof.
If I was not meant to overcome every obstacle put in my
path, then why is it all so *easy*? Anyway, I am blameless.
The pen was held by Rickie's hand and is still now. I see
him in every cafe, at every hotel, under every umbrella I
dodge in every narrow street. He hops on every bus behind
me, collects my tickets on all the trains in each town I find
myself drawn to. If I stumble on my way to cash his
cheque, he helps me to my feet, stills my shaking hand and
fixes my gaze straight ahead even as gravity conspires to
pull my guilty head down down down into the dirt. His
whisper in my ear a caress, a comfort: You are not alone.
You are not alone. You are not. Tom.

Richard *slides the pile of cash over to* **Tom** *and shuts the
cashbox.*

Richard   You are aware, Signor Greenleaf, that your
withdrawal leaves you with very little in this account.

Tom   Oh, yes. I am aware of that. Don't worry. There's
plenty more where that came from. (*Beat.*) I mean, a
deposit is made into the account on the first of each
month. From America. A trust. (*He laughs.*) I'm afraid my
parents think I spend too much money as it is, but I can't
help myself. A man gets to travel freely so rarely, don't you
think? Goodbye, Rickie. See you soon.

Richard   I beg your –

Tom (*interrupts*)   Yes, yes. I know. (*To the audience.*) He begs
my pardon. Wonders never cease. Next stop: American
Express. (*He turns back to* **Richard**.) C'e posta per me? Il
mio nome e Richard Greenleaf. G-R-E-E-N-L –

Richard   Si, signor. Greenleaf. Mister R. Much post for
you.

Richard *gives* **Tom** *a stack of letters.* **Tom** *picks up an ornate
letter opener from the table and rips open one of the letters.* **Herbert**
*enters. He wears yachting clothes and cap and peers through
binoculars.* **Richard** *reads over* **Tom***'s shoulder.*

Herbert   What a relief to finally hear from you, son.
That ditzy girl, what's-her-name-Sherwood, phoned from
Mongibello last month in a panic. Said you'd up and
disappeared to Rome and it just didn't feel right to her, the
way you'd gone. Your mother worried, naturally, but to tell
you the truth, pleasant as this Sherwood seemed, I found
the woman to be hysterical and unreliable. Honestly, I'm
glad you've moved on from her, Richard. Tom Ripley feels
she's entirely too dependent on your good will. By the way,
pleased to hear you get on so well with Tom. He seems to
have worked wonders for your morale and frankly son,
your manners have improved considerably under his
tutelage. Your mother was so very touched to receive your
wonderful gift. I haven't seen her smile like this in years.
But I wish you hadn't spent so much damned money on it.
Anyway, we're off to Cuba or the Bahamas or some
godforsaken sweltering place where your mother insists on
wintering. Keep in touch. And remember: I'll hold you to
that promise of coming home this summer.

Richard   I won't be home this summer, Dad.

Tom   I won't be home at *all*, Dad. Oh well.

Herbert *exits.* **Tom** *shrugs, rips the letter in two, tosses its pieces
into the air.* **Richard** *gives him another letter.* **Emily** *enters.*
Tom *tears open the letter.* **Emily** *wears a swimming costume,
mules, sunglasses, her turban and an incongruous black cashmere scarf.*

Emily   I wear it *everywhere*, darling. I *never* take it off.
Three months since we left New York and counting. I wear
it to breakfast, to the casino, to the beach and to my bed.
At first, your father was charmed by it. But you know him.
Spend a little time in the heat and he loses his sense of
humour. Of course I know I look ridiculous, but it doesn't
matter. From the moment I *touched* your delectable gift, my
health improved. And with each passing day I feel a new
strength gathering. Your father thinks it has to do with
your letters and yes, *of course* they help. Who knew you
were such a prolific writer? And so *witty*. You get it from
me, I'll have you know. Your father is practically illiterate,

he's so inarticulate. But really, darling, I *know* it's the scarf. Believe me. When you've tried as many crackpot cures as I have, you can smell what works and what doesn't.

Emily *exits.*

Richard (*refers to* **Tom**)   Then why can't you sniff this one out, Mother?

Tom (*to* **Richard**)   I do believe my mother's lost her marbles.

Tom *rips up the letter, throws its pieces up into the air. He waits for* **Richard** *to give him another letter.*

Tom   Well. Come on. Don't keep me guessing.

Richard *holds out another letter to* **Tom**. **Tom** *takes it, rips into it with the letter opener.* **Marge** *enters. She wears tennis gear, sports a racquet.*

Marge   Dearest Rickie. Though it pains me to admit this, you were right. Time away from me, from *us*, clearly does you a world of good. Your letters reveal a focus and sensitivity that, frankly, darling, I haven't seen from you since we met. I'm so *proud* of you, Rickie. So happy for your artistic breakthrough. That little watercolour you sent of the Colosseum is *breathtaking*. And if you don't mind me saying so, I think it displays a new maturity in your work.

Tom   The cow doesn't know the difference between one watercolour and the next. I *tried* to imitate your style, Rickie. Really, I did. But it's more difficult than you think to be *truly* untalented. See? Everything I touch turns to gold. Even Marge.

Richard   Marge, I – Marge, please – Marge – MARGE. (*To* **Tom**.) Why can't I say what I want to say? Why won't the words *come*?

Tom   Because the words aren't there. Because the words are *mine*.

Marge   Well, darling, Fausto's waiting on court and I guess I better get out there before he starts without me.

He's got a wicked backhand, you know. *And* he sends his love, as do I. The only thing that could possibly make me happier is knowing when you'll be back. When you'll be *home*. Take care, my darling. Write when you can and please do send more work. It's such a joy to receive. With all my love, I am, as ever.

Tom *starts to rip up the letter.* **Marge** *begins to exit.* **Richard** *tries to grab the letter away from* **Tom** *before* **Tom** *can tear it. They both hold onto one end of the letter, neither willing to give up his end.* **Marge** *stops in her tracks. She looks around as if she heard something moving behind her.*

Marge Fausto? Is that you?

Tom *manages to yank the letter away from* **Richard**. **Marge**, *having had no response, shrugs, exits.*

Richard (*calls after* **Marge**) Marge – MARGE.

But she's gone. **Richard** *sits, defeated again.* **Tom** *rips the letter into precise, small strips. He drops it to the floor.* **Tom** *goes to* **Richard** *as he rips up the letter.*

Tom Look at me.

Richard *looks up at* **Tom**.

Richard Look at you.

Tom *runs his index finger all around* **Richard**'s *face. Then* **Richard** *touches* **Tom**'s *face in the same way.*

Tom See. Isn't this easy?

And without warning, **Tom** *strangles* **Richard**. **Richard** *falls down, dead.* **Tom** *removes a cigarette case from his pocket, lights a cigarette. Then:*

Tom You know, I think I prefer my own brand to yours. It's a surprisingly coarse tobacco, Rickie. Vulgar, even. And here I thought your taste was the standard to which I could only ever *hope* to aspire. I was sorry to kill you, Rickie. At first. I mean – I really *was* fond of you. But the more I learn about your habits, the more I'm convinced I did you

a favour in that boat. You *were* lazy and slovenly. Even
Marge would have given up in disgust at your sloth. And
anyway, your stock has risen greatly since your demise.
People love you, Rickie. They *adore* you now. And tell me
who's made that possible? I haven't lost you, Rickie. You're
just struggling to keep up with me.

Richard *suddenly sits up.* **Tom** *holds out a hand to* **Richard**.

Tom   Here. Grab hold. Let me help you. Again.

The sound of the motorboat is heard coming ever closer. **Richard**
holds out his hand to **Tom**. **Richard** *very nearly manages to grab
hold of* **Tom***'s hand, the motorboat is very close when, like a bolt of
lightning, the motorboat sound is replaced by a loud and insistent
ringing telephone. Lights down very quickly on all but* **Tom** *–
perhaps he's isolated in a tight bright light. Abruptly startled out of
his fantasy,* **Tom** *appears to be, for the first time, thrown by a
situation.*

Tom (*to the audience*)   Can that really be the *telephone*? Such
a common means of communication. And in any case,
nobody has this number. Shall I answer? Shall I let it go?
Such a dangerous decision. Delicious. (*Beat; then, as*
Richard:) Pronto. Sono Greenleaf.

Lights up on **Freddie**.

Freddie   You're a hard man to pin down, Greenleaf. I'll
give you that. Making folks write to you care of American
Express. Unlisted phone number.

Tom   Who is this?

Freddie   Come on, Rickie. You haven't been out of the
loop all *that* long. It's me. Freddie. Freddie *Miles*? Long lost
so-and-so you bumped into not that long ago?

Tom   Ah. Freddie. Of course. (*Beat.*) How did you find
me?

Freddie   Don't sound so thrilled, buddy. I'm around the
corner. Invite me up.

Tom   I – it's not a good time, Freddie. Can I meet you

later on? Say, at three something? We could go to a hotel bar. You'd like that, wouldn't you?

Freddie   Look. I've got to talk to you *now*, Rickie. Like I said, I'm just down the road. I'll be five minutes.

Tom   Well. Okay. If you insist.

Freddie   Now *that's* what I wanna hear. Stay put, friend. I'm on my way.

Light down on **Freddie**.

Tom (*to the audience*)   It was bound to happen. Bumbling hulking *fool* of a man. Always rooting around where he doesn't belong. It's a test. Clearly. But failure is simply not in my cards.

All lights up. **Freddie** *stands before* **Tom**, *hat in hand.*

Freddie   Oh. I didn't know *you* were here. (*Beat.*) Where's Rickie? Back there? Hey, Greenleaf – get your ass in here.

Tom   He's out.

Freddie   That's impossible. He's expecting me.

Tom   I know. He asked me to apologise, but he was called away suddenly.

Freddie   Okay. Where's he gone to? I'll catch up with him. We spoke only a few minutes ago. He can't have got far.

Tom   I'm afraid I can't help you. I'm not in the habit of keeping tabs on Rickie.

Freddie   Didn't ask you if you were. I just wanna know if he told you where he was going.

Tom   Well. No. He didn't.

Freddie   I gotta tell you, I find that pretty strange. I mean, you're having a conversation with somebody, the phone rings, he says sorry buddy – gotta go. And he's gone.

Tom Yes. That's exactly what happened. I don't ask
questions. He was in a hurry. (*Beat.*) You look like you
could use a drink. It's scotch and soda, isn't it?

Freddie I'm not thirsty. (*Beat.*) I guess Marge was right.
This is a pretty nice set-up you've got here. (*Beat.*) Nice girl.
Met her not so long ago in – what's that dopey town called
– Mongibello. Thought I might catch Rickie down there.
(*Beat.*) She told me all about you.

Tom What do you mean?

Freddie Rickie's been keeping a low profile. Avoiding
most of his chums. Doesn't call a soul. That's never been
his style. Common sense dictates there's gotta be a pretty
good reason for a fella changing his behaviour like that. So
I figure, what the hell, I'll drop in to see what makes him
tick these days. And I think I've seen it.

Tom Marge ought to keep her ill-informed opinions to
herself.

Freddie Got nothing to do with Marge.

Tom She told you I was living with Rickie.

Freddie I said no such thing. I *said* she thought you had
a nice set-up. That's different. (*Beat.*) *Are* you living here?

Tom I'm staying here. For the moment. In my own
room.

Freddie You know, that's funny. 'Cause I ran into this
kid downstairs who says Rickie lives here alone and has
done for months. Says he never gets visitors.

Tom I don't think I'd rely on local boys for information
of that sort.

Freddie I didn't say it was a boy.

Tom Didn't you? Well. I assumed. It's not an
unreasonable assumption.

Freddie I don't know about *that*, but, yeah, matter of
fact, it was a boy. And he *works* for Rickie. Silvio. You *do*

know him, don't you?

Tom   I've met him.

Freddie   He's never met you.

Tom   Did you ask him?

Freddie   Well, no, but –

Tom   (*interrupts*)   Now *you're* making assumptions. The fact is, I've been here a very short while. Apparently, Silvio comes in to clean once a fortnight. So he doesn't yet know I'm staying here. But I have met him. Once. I ran into Rickie about a month ago. He was shopping for summer suits. Silvio was helping him carry the packages. I'm sure it wasn't a particularly memorable occasion for him. (*Beat.*) Perhaps you'd be more comfortable waiting in a local cafe. I'm happy to recommend a good one.

Freddie   I think I'll stay, thanks. (*Beat.*) That's a nice jacket.

Tom   Thank you. It's hand-stitched silk and wool.

Freddie   It's also Rickie's fraternity jacket.

Tom   Yes. He graciously allowed me to borrow it.

Freddie   I guess his graciousness knows no bounds as you're wearing his shoes and slacks and belt.

Tom   Shirt and tie, as well. (*Beat.*) My luggage was stolen at the railway station. As I said, I've been here only a short while and until I'm able to arrange for sufficient funds to be wired, Rickie has been generous enough to offer me the pick of his wardrobe.

Freddie   You've got an answer for everything.

Tom   I like to think I'm helpful. (*Beat.*) Would you like to leave a message for Rickie?

Freddie   Herbert Greenleaf sends his regards.

Tom   Oh.

Freddie   Yeah. He seems to think you've been spending quite a bit of time with Rickie. In fact, he's pretty sure you spend most of your time in Rome.

Tom   I can't imagine where he got that impression.

Freddie   From your letters to him.

Tom   I last wrote him some months ago. When I was, indeed, here in Rome. With Rickie. Just after he arrived. I helped him find this apartment. But Mr Greenleaf is not a young man. And perhaps his sense of passing time is not what it used to be.

Freddie   Does Rickie know his father sent you here to bring him back home?

Tom   He is aware of it. Yes.

Freddie   Rickie Greenleaf wouldn't give you the time of day if he knew that.

Tom   You haven't spent any time with Rickie in years. How could you possibly presume to know what he's like?

Freddie   People don't change. They just get worse over time.

Tom   Well. You must be wrong because I'm here, aren't I?

A silence.

Freddie   You know, I think I will go wait in that cafe.

Tom   Yes. That might be for the best. Well. Let's see. The Gedda's an excellent choice. Turn right out of the building, left at the first streetlight, third awning you come to. (*Beat.*) I'm sure Rickie won't be too long. I'll send him along.

Freddie   Sure you will. Oh, by the way, ran into some old Choate buddies couple of weeks back and I was wondering – which house did you live in at school?

Tom   Well, let me think. Isn't that funny? I can't recall the name. It's on the tip of my tongue, though. That wasn't the happiest time of my life. I guess I've blocked it. Momentarily.

Freddie   Yeah, funny how that happens. Maybe I can help you. Was it a brick house or clapboard?

Tom   Brick. Definitely brick.

Freddie   Then that would have been Greenhall House.

Tom   Yes. Greenhall. That's right.

Freddie   Oh, well, I was in Ferrell House. That'll account for it.

Tom   Account for what?

Freddie   Told you the last time. I don't remember you at all. Not from assembly, not from soccer. Not from anywhere.

Tom   I was in the class behind you. We wouldn't have shared assemblies.

Freddie   Can't find you in the yearbooks.

Tom   I was never photographed. Lifelong aversion to cameras.

Freddie (*smiles, ever affable*)   There you go again with the easy answers.

Tom (*shrugs*)   I aim to please.

Freddie   Mr Greenleaf told me how he met you again. After so many years. How he remembered you in goal that day. All bloody and bullied. Quite a story.

Tom   I don't like to be reminded of it. You understand.

Freddie   I sure do. Especially as *I* was the one getting the shit kicked out me in that goal. And you know what else? There is no Greenhall House at Choate.

Tom   Oh dear.

Freddie   Yeah. So. Maybe you wanna tell me what the

hell's been going on here before I lose my patience and call
the cops.

Tom   I wouldn't do that. I really wouldn't even *think*
about it.

Freddie *approaches the table.*

Freddie   You wouldn't? Well, I don't care what *you'd* do.
More I think about it, more it seems like a very fine idea.
Where's the phone?

Tom   Please don't touch what's not yours.

Freddie   You're a fine one to talk.

Freddie *searches for a phone on the table. He finds a stack of
papers. He holds up one sheet. Then another. And another.*

Freddie   What the hell *is* this? There's nothing but
Rickie's signature over and over. On every damned page.

Tom   I told you not to touch anything. Now look what
you've done. Poor Freddie. If only you'd been thirsty and
gone to that cafe like I told you to.

Freddie   I don't really know what you're babbling on
about, but you better start talking something *useful*. Like
where I can find Rickie. Right now.

Tom   Well, Freddie, I'm afraid Rickie's dead. Drowned.
Or, I should say, *bludgeoned* and then drowned.

Freddie   What kind of sick joke –

Tom   Oh, it's not funny. I assure you. It was hard work.
But you'll be pleased to know that his brilliant efforts at the
wing position during his formative years made it very
difficult for me to actually, finally *kill* him. His lung
capacity was truly amazing.

Freddie   *What*? What are you – don't give me *that*. You
haven't got the guts to do something like – like – listen. I
know you've *stolen* from Rickie, cheated his family for sure,
and maybe you've kidnapped him, locked him up
someplace for future –

Tom For future *what*? Please. Give me more credit than that. *Kidnapping*? How pedestrian do you think I am? You really mustn't like me, Freddie.

Freddie *makes a grab for* **Tom**. **Tom** *picks up the letter opener and stabs* **Freddie** *cleanly through the chest.* **Tom** *steps back, well out of* **Freddie**'s *way.*

Tom If you doubted I had the guts to murder before, you certainly can't doubt it now. Because I seem to have *your* guts well in hand.

Tom *laughs.* **Freddie** *manages to stumble forward for a few steps before he falls, quite dead.*

Tom Poor dumb Freddie. You let some misplaced sentimental notion of friendship kill you. I could have saved you the trouble. Rickie barely remembered you. And where did it get you?

Tom *pokes at* **Freddie**'s *side with the tip of his shoe.*

Tom Pathetic beached whale of an *excuse* for a man. Look at you. Bleeding all over my carpet. Look. LOOK. (*Beat.*) WHAT DID YOU MAKE ME DO. WHAT. WHAT.

Tom, *in a frenzy, kicks* **Freddie**'s *body repeatedly.*

Tom (*as he kicks* **Freddie**'s *body*) Stupid stupid stupid BASTARD want to wish to NEED to RUIN things for me but no no no NO it's not to BE it's not your PLACE it's your own damned stupid stupid FAULT you end up DEAD and I never never never NEVER LOSE MY TEMPER NEVER MAKE ME NEVER TELL ME WHAT TO –

Tom, *exhausted, hyperventilating, realising what he's done, steps back and away from the body. He shuts his eyes as if to rid himself of the body.*

Tom I don't want to see. I mustn't see. Please *please* don't make me see.

And just like that, the light disappears from **Freddie**'s *body.* **Tom** *opens his eyes.* **Freddie** *is no longer there.* **Tom** *struggles to catch his breath.*

Tom Good. That's . . . good. Come . . . on . . . Breathe. Breathe. Yes. That's . . . that's . . . *it.* Yessss. Breathe. Deep. Deeper. Ah. Oh. Yes.

And all at once, the peaceful sound of the gulls and gentle waves and ship bells fill the air. **Tom** *breathes deeply – in and out, in and out.*

Tom (*to the audience*) Disposing of Freddie Miles is a nightmare. Even in death, he's a problem. But fortunately, he had a car. Lazy and unimaginative men always drive.

Throughout the following, **Tom** *opens the suitcase, takes out his original clothing, lays it all out neatly. He undresses and carefully re-clothes himself in his old stuff. He folds and packs* **Richard**'s *clothing into the suitcase. He repositions the parting in his hair so that it's back to* **Tom**'s *original style.*

Tom By the time I manage to drag his carcass out the front door it's pitch black. How do I know I won't see a soul along the way? I simply do. (*Beat.*) He just about fits in the trunk. What is the most fitting death for Freddie Miles – I ask myself. Not peacefully, in his sleep, devoted but dim wife by his side. No no no – no rest for the wicked. And certainly not heroically – no soldiers or firemen or good samaritans in Freddie's future. What *does* he deserve? And then it occurs to me. Plain as day. He is viciously stabbed and beaten to death in a robbery. He's drunk and loud and all-too complicit in his own destruction. *That's* what he deserves. And this is how it shall be: I take his wallet, his car keys and dump him behind a headstone along the Appian Way. He'll be found within days. Or hours. Or weeks. No matter. It's undignified. That's the important thing. (*Beat.*) Rickie stops writing to his parents. To Marge. Is it a coincidence? Or is it somehow tied to Freddie Miles's disappearance? Who can say for sure? Speculation is useless. It's better to wait for answers. They'll find you. (*Beat.*) Of course, police involvement is inevitable.

Tom's *transformation is accomplished. He looks exactly as he did at* *the beginning of the play. He snaps shut the suitcase as* **Tenente Roverini** *enters.* **Roverini** *carries a notebook in which he occasionally writes or consults.*

Roverini   And that was this past Tuesday, Signor Reeplay? Or the previous Tuesday?

Tom   Ripley. The previous Tuesday. Yes.

Roverini   Yes. This makes sense. The last time you saw Signor Greenleaf was the evening of Signor Miles's murder. This makes sense.

Tom   Of course, I might be mistaken. I'd been to Milan, you see, all of the previous week and had only just returned to Rome. I was exhausted from my trip. I trade in a highly competitive business, you see. You may wish to verify the details of my trip with Rickie's valet.

Roverini   This would be . . . Silvio Ferrante, yes?

Tom   I believe that's his name. I knew him only as Silvio.

Roverini   Seems he has taken employment somewhere in the north. Venice, Verona – who knows? We've yet to trace him. But . . . we are confident.

Tom   I'm glad to hear that. I feel sure he could help your investigation.

Roverini   Did you know him well?

Tom   Oh, no. Not at all, in fact. He was a servant.

Roverini (*shrugs*)   You might say *I* am a servant. (*Beat.*) But, no – I meant Signor Miles. Did you know *him* well?

Tom   Freddie? No. Not really. In fact, I'd never met him. (*Beat.*) Oh – hold on. Once. Yes, I met him once. When we were staying in Mongibello. Rickie and I took a short trip to Rome and we ran into Freddie, I don't know, in a bar or a cafe. He was pretty high. On a business trip, something like that.

Roverini *jots down a few lines, consults previous notes.*

Roverini   The friend to Signor Greenleaf, Signorina
Sherwood, yes? She tells me you and Signor Miles and
Signor Greenleaf all went to the same school. So she must
be mistaken, no?

Tom   No. We did. Go to the same school. Definitely.

Roverini   But how can it be that you never met Signor
Miles before you – how you say? – run *into* him – with
Signor Greenleaf? If you went to the same school, how can
this be?

Tom   I was in the class behind Rickie and Freddie Miles.
So we never met, Freddie and me. I *saw* him, of course
but, as I said . . . well, there wasn't much interaction
between the different grades at our school. (*Beat.*) You don't
think *Rickie* had anything to do with Freddie's, well, I don't
like to *say* it even.

Roverini   I would not like to say it, either.

Tom   But you're thinking about Rickie. As a suspect, I
mean.

Roverini   I would not wish that on a friend, Signor
Ripley.

Tom   You misunderstand. I don't wish it. I fear it. I fear
for Rickie.

Roverini   Yes, yes. This makes sense.

Roverini *scribbles in his notebook.*

Tom   All I meant to say was, well, Freddie's been
murdered and Rickie's disappeared. I'm concerned that
there might be a link. Though I refuse to believe there is.

Roverini   You seem not at all concerned with the fate of
Signor Greenleaf.

Tom   Of course I am. Nobody wants to think of their
friends as criminals.

Roverini   Perhaps Signor Greenleaf is hurt, suffering from
– who knows? – amnesia? Or perhaps he is dead. (*Beat.*)

You don't seem to have considered that possibility.

Tom Oh my. (*Beat.*) No. I hadn't.

Tom *takes out his cigarette case, lights a cigarette.*

Tom The thought of Rickie being dead is even more shocking than the thought of his being a murderer. I somehow just can't bring myself to – cigarette?

Tom *holds out the case to* **Roverini**.

Roverini Grazie, no. I am the only man in Rome who refuses a good smoke. I love to be around it, but ... my lungs, they are genetically indisposed to tobacco.

Tom What a pity.

Tom *starts to put the case away.*

Roverini But the case – it is very beautiful. May I?

Tom Of course.

Tom *gives* **Roverini** *the cigarette case.*

Roverini Emphysema, tuberculosis, asthma, bronchitis – you name an affliction of the chest or lung, it runs in my family. None of us can be relied upon to draw a decent breath from one moment to the next. If one can't inhale, one might as well surround oneself with the trappings of smoke. So I collect. Cases are my speciality. This one is – yes, yes. Very unusual. Delicate. Hand-beaten metal. Very old.

Tom *checks his watch.*

Roverini Are you in a hurry, Signor Ridley?

Tom Oh – no, no. Not at all. I was just –

Roverini No, no – don't apologise. Why, you must think, is this crazy old cop wasting your time with this and that about ... this and that?

Tom Well, now that you mention it –

Roverini (*as he holds the cigarette case up to the light*) Lovely detailing. An absolute gem. I bet you picked this up at auction, no?

Tom   Sotheby's. I think. Or it might have been Christie's. Can't remember.

Roverini   Yes, yes. An auction makes sense. If you don't mind my asking, what was its cost?

Tom   Fifty. Or a hundred, maybe. Sorry. It was a while back and I'm not very good with that sort of detail.

Roverini   Well, I have *heard* of bargains at auction, but this . . . this is – how you say? – a steal.

Tom   I'm lucky. I guess.

Roverini   Luck. Yes, yes. Makes sense. Makes – ah. Look here. In the corner of the case, a very delicate engraving. Some initials I can't quite make out but – oh yes. I see it now. R-H-G.

Tom   A silversmith's mark.

Roverini   No, no – *that* I find already. No. This is something, I think maybe – yes, yes. These initials, I am sure they are personalised. For the owner of the case.

Tom   How interesting.

Roverini   Oh, no. It's not. I mean, the case, it is old. It has possibly had many owners and it is not at all unusual for – but. Maybe – no. No. Surely not. Let me just – Here, signor. Take your case. Grazie.

Roverini *gives* **Tom** *the cigarette case.* **Roverini** *consults his notebook. He flips backwards and forward through its pages.*

Tom   I don't mean to be rude, but I *am* late for an appointment, to tell you the truth.

Roverini   This is a strange turn of phrase: to tell you the truth. I find when people say it, they mean nothing of the sort. (*Beat.*) Here. I knew I had written it somewhere. Herbert Greenleaf. Yes. I thought it might be.

Tom   Rickie's father.

Roverini   Very pleasant man. Of course, I have never met him. Just several telephone conversations, but one can make certain character judgments, nonetheless. Decent man. Honest. You have met him, no?

Tom   Once or twice. What about him?

Roverini   R-H-G. Richard Herbert Greenleaf. Was that Signor Greenleaf's full name?

Tom   I haven't the slightest idea.

Roverini   But it is possible, yes? Given his father's name?

Tom   I suppose. Look. Why don't you simply phone Herbert Greenleaf and ask him?

Tom *puts out his cigarette as if to punctuate the end of their conversation.*

Roverini   I shall. (*Beat.*) The initials on your cigarette case, Signor Ringley. Are they a coincidence?

Tom   What *is* your problem with my name? (*Beat.*) Of course it's a coincidence. The case is hundreds of years old. You said so yourself. Anyway, what else would it be other than coincidence?

Roverini (*shrugs*)   You are a lucky man.

Tom   Not especially.

Roverini (*consults his notes*)   No? I could have sworn – yes, yes. Here it is. (*He quotes* **Tom**.) 'I am lucky'. You said it not five minutes ago.

Tom   All right. So I said I was lucky. What of it?

Roverini   Luck follows coincidence and vice versa. That is all. (*Beat.*) In any case, my inquiries complete, it seems clearer to me that Signor Miles's luck ran out when he last came in contact with Signor Greenleaf. It is difficult to draw another conclusion, however hard I look for one.

Tom   I'm sure Rickie will turn up. And then all will be explained.

Roverini   Do you think?

Tom   Yes. Sooner or later. In some . . . circumstance . . . or other.

The sound of the motorboat is heard – but it's indistinct, far away, nearly unrecognizable.

Roverini   Yes, yes. This makes sense.

Roverini *packs his notebook and pen away in his pocket.*

Tom   Do you think?

A pause. The sound of the motorboat draws nearer. **Tom** *smiles, holds out his hand to shake* **Roverini***'s hand.* **Roverini** *hesitates slightly before shaking* **Tom***'s hand. Then:*

Roverini (*refers to the suitcases*)   Are you planning a trip?

Tom   I was. I am. Venice.

Roverini   Oh, Venezia. Stunning. Such light. Shadow. And the Lido – you really must try the Venetian beaches. They are an acquired taste, but when you acquire the taste, well. There's nothing like it.

Tom   I'm not one for beaches. Or water, for that matter.

Roverini   Then Venice is an unfortunate choice, no?

The motorboat sound grows ever closer and speedier.

Tom   Not really. One need never set foot in Venetian waters. Boats, Tenente Roverini, hide a multitude of sins.

Richard *enters. He is dressed exactly as he was when* **Tom** *murdered him except that all of his clothes are now white – including shoes, belt, and any accessories. He listens to the sound of the motorboat. His breathing becomes shallow; towards the end of* **Tom***'s speech he begins to hyperventilate.*

Roverini (*shrugs*)   Still. It is a pity to fear the water. Without it, we do not exist. (*Beat.*) How you say? – I'll be in touch. Signor Ripley.

Roverini *exits. The motorboat picks up yet more speed, grows closer and closer.* **Richard** *drops to his knees, unable to stand the sound. He puts his hands over his ears, rocks back and forth.* **Tom** *approaches him.* **Tom** *stands quite still, watching* **Richard** *as if he's some kind of experiment. He lights a cigarette.*

Tom   But he isn't in touch because he finds nothing. No Rickie, no Massimo, nothing. Every direction he takes finds a dead end and every direction I take finds an open door, an answered question. (*Beat.*) Of course, it is a nuisance not being able to cash any more of your cheques. But. For every action there is an equal and positive reaction – isn't that right? And in the end, I can't complain. Venice is cold, Rickie. Anonymous. No chance of discovery. Glorious. (*Beat.*) I'll miss you. Despite your shortcomings, you're good company.

Tom *bends to touch* **Richard***'s shoulder. As he touches* **Richard***, the motorboat sound cuts out and* **Richard** *immediately begins to breathe more easily.*

Tom   It's time.

Richard   What time is it?

Tom *offers his cigarette to* **Richard***.*

Tom   What's yours is mine.

Richard *takes the cigarette. He inhales gratefully.*

Richard   What's mine is yours. (*Beat.*) What time is it?

Tom   Half past. Quarter to. On the hour. High noon.

Richard   Is that the time? I thought it was twenty of. Three minutes after. Eleven seventeen and fifty –

Tom *silences* **Richard** *by touching his index finger to* **R**— *lips.* **Tom** *takes the cigarette from* **Richard** *and puts* **Tom** *takes* **Richard***'s hands in his own hands. T*— *other. The sound of the gulls, the waves, the gentle s*—

Tom   I might get seasick.

Richard   Has it happened to you befo—

Tom   No. But it might.

Richard   I won't let you be sick. I'll protect you, Tom.

Tom   I'd like that. (*Beat.*) I love the sea. You've made me love the sea.

Richard   Tom, this is kinda – hell, it's *really* awkward, but I gotta ask – I gotta take this chance –

Tom   Ask me anything.

Richard   I mean, why put off the inevitable? I think you and me, we've been headed this way for some time. We have this joke, you and me, that we'll live happily ever after, mostly under cover.

Tom   Yes. We do.

Richard   You've made me think long and hard about the choices I've made. Who knows. Maybe I'll even learn to like my dad and his shipyard. Maybe you and my mom will become bridge partners.

Tom   I doubt very much whether your mother and I will become bosom pals. I didn't like to tell you, Rickie, but your mother. She's dying. A terrible cancer. Quite inoperable. And your father's given up on you, so I wouldn't bother harbouring any residual feelings about the family business. I'm afraid I'm all you have left.

Richard   That's as it should be. That's – it leads me to – what I wanted to say before, well, I don't know how –

Tom   Are you asking me to marry you?

Richard   I guess I am. Yeah.

Tom   Men don't marry each other. What a preposterous suggestion.

Richard   I love you. I have always loved you. From the moment I saw you. From the moment we met.

Richard *pulls* **Tom** *close to him and kisses him – a long, deep, ⟨shoc⟩kingly sensual kiss.* **Richard** *breaks off the kiss.*

Richard   What have I done. I've ruined everything.

Tom   Yes. You have. (*Beat.*) What will you do now?

Richard   There's nothing left *to* do. (*Beat.*) You've been so good to me, Tom. And I've repaid your kindness with weakness. Dishonesty. Tell me. Please. How can I help myself?

Tom   Through pain. Misery. And deep, deep suffering. Will you do this for me?

Richard   Yes. For you. Always.

Richard *removes a folded document from his pocket, a will – perhaps tied together with a little red ribbon – and gives it to* **Tom**, *who lovingly puts it in his own pocket.*

Tom *rises.* **Richard** *rises.* **Tom** *gives* **Richard** *the suitcase.*

Tom   Are you going to jump?

Richard   I'm gonna jump. Watch me jump.

Tom   Will I be able to steer the boat?

Richard   Sure. Just make sure the compass points north. Always north.

Tom   I wish there was another way.

Marge *enters. She's somewhat drunk. She wears slacks which are rolled up to her knees. She carries her shoes. She walks as if she's walking through water.*

Marge (*she giggles*)   Are you *sure* there isn't another way into your palazzo? Dontcha keep a key under some kinda, I don't know, big *stone* or something? I guess it's my fault 'cause I just *had* to go and make the boat drop us at the back canal. So much for romance. Stupid, stupid me. But – gosh, Tom. I still can't believe you've got your very own Venetian palazzo. It's thrilling. It's like *Hollywood*.

Richard   This is the only way. Watch me, now. Watch me swim away.

Tom   I'm watching. There you go. You're swimming. You're fine.

Richard   Watch me, Tom. Keep watching me.

And **Richard** *exits.* **Tom** *looks after him.*

Tom   I couldn't have stopped you even if I wanted to.

A moment, then **Tom** *takes off his shoes and rolls up his trouser legs to just above his knees.*

Marge (*she giggles again*)   I mean, *really*, Tom. Who would have thought art dealing or stealing or *whatever* it is you do could be so lucrative? Mind you – my Mongibello book's made me a tidy sum. I guess I have Rickie's watercolours to thank for that. It's a good thing I used them to illustrate it rather than my own half-assed photographs. (*Beat.*) Isn't that weird?

Tom *enters the scene with* **Marge**.

Tom   What's weird about it?

Marge   He always thought he was so untalented. (*Beat.*) When the Greenleafs contacted me last year, I felt as if I couldn't breathe. As if my lungs had collapsed and there was no possibility for air to reach me in time. I mean, it had been some time since Rickie disappeared. But suicide. I wasn't expecting it. None of us was, I suppose.

Tom   No. I suppose not. (*Beat.*) I had hoped that Rickie would turn up one day, a knock at my door and there he'd stand, sunburnt and peeling and smiling like he always was.

Marge   Well. I guess I kinda hoped he'd show up at my door first.

A silence. They slosh around in the water.

Tom   I hate these canals. Full of sludge and slime and God knows what else. What the – ouch – something's, I don't know – something's got my *leg*.

Marge *bends down to inspect* **Tom**'s *leg. She begins to giggle.*

Marge   Oh, Tom, lemme see – give your leg here –

gosh, it's *dark*. Can't see a blasted thing without – it's just algae or seaweed or some damn thing's wrapped round your leg it's nothing to worry about and – oops. Now look what I've done. I've fallen.

Marge *falls into the water. She has a giggling fit that becomes a coughing fit as she swallows water.*

Marge   Tom – Tom you gotta – it's just so *funny* – Tom. Tom. Please you gotta – come on I can't – breathe – I can't – TOM. TOM. TAKE MY HAND.

Marge *is really beginning to choke. She reaches a hand out to* **Tom**. **Tom** *watches her for a moment as if she's a bug or something pinned under a microscope. He bends down, finally, to take her hand and pull her up out of the water.*

Tom   It's not very deep here. Just a foot or two.

Marge   Well it's probably enough to drown in. Christ. *That* sobered me up. Thanks, a bunch, Tom. You're a real lifesaver.

Tom   I found a key. On the step where you fell. Isn't that lucky? Let's go inside. Where it's warm. I'll fix us some brandies.

Tom *turns to exit.*

Marge   I know how much he meant to you, Tom. And I mean that sincerely. No rancour. No bitterness. He would have wanted that from us both. (*Beat.*) I'm going back to Boston, you know.

Tom   That's brave of you. I suppose.

Marge   It's exciting. And, yes, I guess it's a little scary. I mean, the book's going to be published there. Can you imagine? Marge Sherwood published in *America*? I walk around with my eyes shut tight for fear that if I open them, my good fortune will disappear.

Tom   I'm sure it won't. (*Beat.*) You know, Marge, I really don't think you would have drowned on the steps. Your head was never below the water. (*Beat.*) Ah. Here we go.

The spare key worked and all is well with the world. After you.

Tom *steps aside and motions for* **Marge** *to step inside his villa.* **Herbert** *enters. He wears a coat and hat – winter gear. He sits at the table.*

Herbert   He left it to us to decide. We thought it best – well, it was Emily's idea, really – to give you all of it. The stock, the cash, the bonds. His clothes, even. She felt it was what he would have wanted. Considering. Well, you know. It's hard for me to talk about it even now.

Marge *giggles, bows to* **Tom**.

Marge   Why, thank you kind sir. Such a gentleman. A prince among men. That's what I've *always* said about you, Tom Ripley.

Tom   Indeed.

He smiles at **Marge** *as she exits, stumbling. The water sounds gradually disappear through* **Herbert***'s speech.*

Herbert   I mean, we *thought* about giving the lot to charity. We really did. But Emily was right. Rickie would never have given a penny to charity, much as I don't care to admit it. My son was not a generous soul.

Tom   He wasn't unkind.

Herbert   No. No, I guess not. At least, he had a soft spot for you. (*Beat.*) We *did* wait before executing his wishes. God knows why. I mean, it wasn't as if he was going to return from – well. Without a body, you see. There was still. Perhaps. (*Beat.*) Anyway. He left it to us to decide what you got and we decided to give you the lot.

Tom   I can't let you do that.

Herbert   You can. And you will. Before Emily died she made it clear that it was the least we could do in order to make up for – to compensate you in some way for – Look. I do not begin to fathom the reasons for Richard's behaviour. It's hard to believe he killed a man. But I guess once you come to terms with something like that, it's easy to believe anything.

Tom   I believe Rickie was a good man, Mister Greenleaf.

Herbert   Do you? Do you really?

Tom   Yes. Most definitely.

Herbert   Thank you for that.

A silence.

Tom   Did Mrs Greenleaf . . . go . . . peacefully?

Herbert   She woke up one night in a panic while I was away on business. It must have been a nightmare. Or a hallucination. Towards the end, the drugs she took – believe me, they could have a pretty powerful effect on her mind – well. We kept a bell on her bedside table. So she could ring for me or for the nurse – we kept a nurse round the clock these last few months – and I guess she'd forgotten where she'd put the damned bell so she got up and for some reason didn't bother to put on a light – that's why I think it must have been a nightmare that woke her, you see, because she'd have been afraid and not thinking about things like light or or – well. She must have just thrown open the bedroom door and made for the stairs because that's where the nurse found her. At the bottom of the stairs. She'd tripped over the bell which had been left lying at the top of the stairs. (*Beat.*) She'd get so lonely without me sometimes she'd. She'd sit huddled at the top of the stairs waiting for me to come home. Wrapped in blankets. Clutching that bell.

A silence. **Herbert** *looks around.*

Herbert   This is quite a place.

Tom   A devil to heat.

Herbert   I bet it is. (*Beat.*) I don't know why I felt I had to do this personally. But I simply had to. You understand.

Tom   Yes. I do.

Herbert   The thing is, the thing I can't seem to wrap my mind around is, towards the end, you know, towards Richard's . . . end . . . he wrote to us so much more than he ever did before. I felt he was finally maturing. That he really did love us. Or at least appreciate us. Something. There was *something* between us, don't you think?

Tom   I know there was.

Herbert   Yes. Well. (*Beat.*) I'm sorry. But I have nothing else to say. This happens to me nowadays. I just . . . run out of conversation. And then I have to leave.

Herbert *rises.*

Herbert   Goodbye, Tom. Please don't think me rude if I ask you not to be in touch with me again.

Tom   Of course not.

They shake hands.

Herbert   My lawyer will contact you with the details of the transfers. Yes. Well. That's it, then.

A brief silence. Neither man moves. Finally, **Herbert** *shrugs, tips his hat to* **Tom***, and exits.*

Tom (*he addresses the audience*)   And so, I find myself alone. Finally, blissfully, *alone*. Listen. Can't you hear the silence? Can't you hear the *motion* of the silence? The water, well, that was the easiest to block out. That went first. Other noise – people, animals, music – that's much harder. But I'm working on it. Oh, yes. I am. And I know I'll get there in the end. Already there are these moments. Listen. *Listen.* It's exquisite, this silence. This peace. (*Beat.*) And I know I'll get there in the end. I'll get there. And when I do, I'll be flying. I'll be. I'll.

Aunt Dottie *enters and strides purposefully up to* **Tom***. She slips her arm through his.* **Tom** *stares straight ahead, as if he doesn't even hear her. He's miles away.*

Aunt Dottie   *There* you are. Honestly, Tom, one minute you're next to me looking at some religious *fresco* or other

and the next minute I turn around and you've vanished.
Lucky for me a very nice young Roman Catholic Italian
priest noticed you'd come up here. (*Beat.*) Don't you think
it's more than a little frightening all this way up? I mean,
what do you see up here except a lot of bland blue Italian
sky? (*Beat.*) Oh – how could I forget to tell you – that *awful*
fat little friend of yours – what's his name – Priminger –
there was a terrible scandal with the police. Some kind of
tax fraud and well, they arrested *him* for it, good Lord, and
all the papers said his trial was the most sensational in
memory. His deception was that good. But not good
enough, evidently, because he was locked away for so many
years he'll be dead before he gets out. (*Beat.*) Do you know
what this reminds me of, being all the way up here? When
I was a young girl – and yes, Tom, there *was* a time when
I really was young – my parents took me one summer to
Cape Cod. Martha's Vineyard. It was deserted in those
days. Desolate. But beautiful. And early one morning, I
crept out along the beach and walked such a long way my
legs ached and I grew very tired. I was lost. With nothing
behind or ahead of me but endless sea and sand. I rubbed
my eyes as if to scrub away my fear, and when I opened
them again there stood not five feet away from me an
enormous pier. And this pier rose so high out of the water
that I had to bend my neck all the way back in order to
see to the top. And there, at the top of that pier, sat two
young men and a woman. Stark naked. They sat at a
perfectly laid table eating breakfast. Toast and marmalade.
(*Beat.*) I felt I should run from them, hide, and so I ran
beneath that pier. I looked up and could see the three of
them between the cracks in the wooden planks. I touched a
plank and for some reason I have never understood, I
began to cry. And cry. My tears simply would not stop.
And then, without warning, the pier began to sink. Very
quickly. It slid silently into the sand beneath the water. I
tried to hold it up. I did. But I was so young, you see, and
not very strong. And of course, I couldn't *see* through all
my tears. (*Beat.*) I barely got out from under in time to see
the whole thing simply . . . vanish. Under water. And those

three people sat there eating breakfast. Throughout it all. Quite calmly. As they went under, I noticed the woman take a bite of the toast. And the toast burst into flames. And after that ... bubbles. And then. Nothing. (*Beat.*) I never told my parents. (*Beat.*) I have never been so thrilled or so frightened in my life. Until now. This height. The sky. Something reminds me of it. And I can't say what. *Why* can't I say what? (*Beat.*) Tom? Tom? Honestly, you exasperate me. Have you heard a single word I've said to you? Tom. Tom. (*Beat.*) TOM.

But **Tom** *has not wavered. He stares out, far away from her. A smile spreads across his face. He closes his eyes. It's bliss, the silence. It goes on. And on.*

Blackout.

A SELECTED LIST OF
METHUEN MODERN PLAYS

☐	CLOSER	Patrick Marber	£6.99
☐	THE BEAUTY QUEEN OF LEENANE	Martin McDonagh	£6.99
☐	A SKULL IN CONNEMARA	Martin McDonagh	£6.99
☐	THE LONESOME WEST	Martin McDonagh	£6.99
☐	THE CRIPPLE OF INISHMAAN	Martin McDonagh	£6.99
☐	THE STEWARD OF CHRISTENDOM	Sebastian Barry	£6.99
☐	SHOPPING AND F***ING	Mark Ravenhill	£6.99
☐	FAUST (FAUST IS DEAD)	Mark Ravenhill	£5.99
☐	POLYGRAPH	Robert Lepage and Marie Brassard	£6.99
☐	BEAUTIFUL THING	Jonathan Harvey	£6.99
☐	MEMORY OF WATER & FIVE KINDS OF SILENCE	Shelagh Stephenson	£7.99
☐	WISHBONES	Lucinda Coxon	£6.99
☐	BONDAGERS & THE STRAW CHAIR	Sue Glover	£9.99
☐	SOME VOICES & PALE HORSE	Joe Penhall	£7.99
☐	KNIVES IN HENS	David Harrower	£6.99
☐	BOYS' LIFE & SEARCH AND DESTROY	Howard Korder	£8.99
☐	THE LIGHTS	Howard Korder	£6.99
☐	SERVING IT UP & A WEEK WITH TONY	David Eldridge	£8.99
☐	INSIDE TRADING	Malcolm Bradbury	£6.99
☐	MASTERCLASS	Terrence McNally	£5.99
☐	EUROPE & THE ARCHITECT	David Grieg	£7.99
☐	BLUE MURDER	Peter Nichols	£6.99
☐	BLASTED & PHAEDRA'S LOVE	Sarah Kane	£7.99

• All Methuen Drama books are available through mail order or from your local bookshop.

Please send cheque/eurocheque/postal order (sterling only) Access, Visa, Mastercard, Diners Card, Switch or Amex.

☐☐☐☐☐☐☐☐☐☐☐☐☐☐☐☐

Expiry Date:_____Signature: _____

Please allow 75 pence per book for post and packing U.K.
Overseas customers please allow £1.00 per copy for post and packing.

ALL ORDERS TO:

Methuen Books, Books by Post, TBS Limited, The Book Service, Colchester Road, Frating Green, Colchester, Essex CO7 7DW.

NAME: _____

ADDRESS: _____

_____

Please allow 28 days for delivery. Please tick box if you do not
wish to receive any additional information ☐

Prices and availability subject to change without notice.

METHUEN SCREENPLAYS

☐ BEAUTIFUL THING	Jonathan Harvey	£6.99
☐ THE ENGLISH PATIENT	Anthony Minghella	£7.99
☐ THE CRUCIBLE	Arthur Miller	£6.99
☐ THE WIND IN THE WILLOWS	Terry Jones	£7.99
☐ PERSUASION	Jane Austen, adapted by Nick Dear	£6.99
☐ TWELFTH NIGHT	Shakespeare, adapted by Trevor Nunn	£7.99
☐ THE KRAYS	Philip Ridley	£7.99
☐ THE AMERICAN DREAMS (THE REFLECTING SKIN & THE PASSION OF DARKLY NOON)	Philip Ridley	£8.99
☐ MRS BROWN	Jeremy Brock	£7.99
☐ THE GAMBLER	Dostoyevsky, adapted by Nick Dear	£7.99
☐ TROJAN EDDIE	Billy Roche	£7.99
☐ THE WINGS OF THE DOVE	Hossein Amini	£7.99
☐ THE ACID HOUSE TRILOGY	Irvine Welsh	£8.99
☐ THE LONG GOOD FRIDAY	Barrie Keeffe	£6.99
☐ SLING BLADE	Billy Bob Thornton	£7.99

- All Methuen Drama books are available through mail order or from your local bookshop.

Please send cheque/eurocheque/postal order (sterling only) Access, Visa, Mastercard, Diners Card, Switch or Amex.

☐☐☐☐☐☐☐☐☐☐☐☐☐☐☐☐

Expiry Date: _____ Signature: _____

Please allow 75 pence per book for post and packing U.K.
Overseas customers please allow £1.00 per copy for post and packing.

ALL ORDERS TO:

Methuen Books, Books by Post, TBS Limited, The Book Service, Colchester Road, Frating Green, Colchester, Essex CO7 7DW.

NAME: _____

ADDRESS: _____

_____

Please allow 28 days for delivery. Please tick box if you do not
wish to receive any additional information ☐

Prices and availability subject to change without notice.

For a Complete Catalogue of Methuen Drama titles
write to:

Methuen Drama
20 Vauxhall Bridge Road
London SW1V 2SA